Douglas H Rhoades

LABELS, LEADVILLE AND LORE

DOUGLAS H. RHOADES

TRADE MARK.

CALIFORNIA FRUITS
SAN JOSE FRUIT PACKING CO.
SAN JOSE CAL. U.S.A.

BOSTON BAKED BEANS
PATENTED AUG. 7TH 1877.
W. K. LEWIS
BOSTON.

1870's—1890's
HISTORY
FROM A
TIN CAN

I

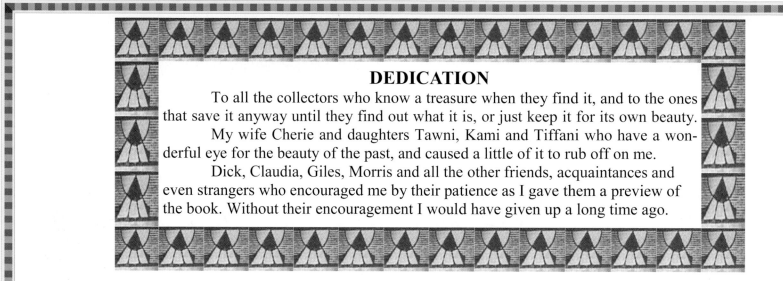

DEDICATION

To all the collectors who know a treasure when they find it, and to the ones that save it anyway until they find out what it is, or just keep it for its own beauty.

My wife Cherie and daughters Tawni, Kami and Tiffani who have a wonderful eye for the beauty of the past, and caused a little of it to rub off on me.

Dick, Claudia, Giles, Morris and all the other friends, acquaintances and even strangers who encouraged me by their patience as I gave them a preview of the book. Without their encouragement I would have given up a long time ago.

LABELS, LEADVILLE AND LORE

Copyright 2005 by Douglas H. Rhoades

Rhoades Publishing

(360) 568-8838
www.labelsandlore.com
E-mail   book@labelsandlore.com

Library of Congress Control Number: 2005901770
ISBN 0-615-12816-5
First Edition
Printed in the U. S. A.

CREDITS & ACKNOWLEDGMENTS

Photography unless otherwise noted   Kory Rhoades
Editing   Cherie Rhoades
Technical support   Kelly Rhoades
Digitally restored Labels   Carolyn Wheeler
Photograph on Page V courtesy of "Antiques Roadshow"/WGBH Boston.

I thank Beth and Bill Sagstetter for photographing the first cans before we knew anything about them except that they were old. Later I was able to clean another layer of dirt from the labels requiring new photographs to be taken.

Thanks to the staff of the Antiques Roadshow, especially Rudy Franchi, Simeon Lipman and Ines Hofmann for their enthusiasm that gave credibility to these wonderful old labels.

I appreciate the help I received from those working at the Engineering Library of the University of Washington, during research of the U. S. Patent books for trademarks. Other libraries researched include Lake County, Colorado, Weber County, Utah, and Lynnwood and Everett, Washington.

Without the encouragement from Dr. Lorne Hammond and Dr. Robert Griffin, of The Royal B. C. Museum, concerning the historical significance of these labels, the book would probably never have been written.

I thank my family who have listened to the 'can' story for years as I told anyone else who would listen, including the many guests of The Ice Palace Inn Bed & Breakfast who heard the history during breakfast.

Thanks to Ted Wiswell for the old Leadville prints.

ABOUT THE AUTHOR AND COMMENTS

Doug was born and raised in Grand Junction, Colorado, where he grew up on five acres in the house his parents, Bill and Vera, built with their two boys. His father worked for the Denver & Rio Grande Western Railroad and loved to travel, sometimes by train, but mostly by car all over North America. His parents traveled with Doug and his older brother Frank to every state, visiting historic places and museums as they went. (Pages 184 & 185)

Doug's early life helped set the stage for his interest in old things and 'found' treasures. Growing up in Western Colorado placed him close to the dinosaur finds and early American artifacts of the West. Countless memorable days, over many years, were spent searching the mountains and deserts for treasures with the hope of finding anything worth telling about. Art and architecture were studied at Mesa College in Grand Junction, Colorado.

Doug comes from a line of determined men who set their minds to something and accomplished it, whether they were building their own homes or helping families stranded on snowy mountain roads, similar to his ancestors when they helped rescue the Donner Party in 1847.

Forty two years of marriage, five children and the responsibilities of family life slowed down any concentrated efforts of treasure hunting. It was during the years 1972 to 1984 of restoring homes in Salem, Oregon, Doug realized how much history was contained in the hidden areas of these older homes. In 1976 he purchased an 1894 Victorian home for one dollar, dismantled the second floor, had it moved four miles, and then put it back together. Remodeling and restoring older homes became an accidental treasure hunt.

He has continually taken on projects no one else wanted, and after moving back to Leadville he became known as the contractor who could put a foundation under any existing home. This line of work led to the discovery of the tin cans, which in turn led to writing this book to preserve this important segment of history.

Throughout his life he has had an ease with people and can talk to anyone. Doug enjoys sailing with family and friends and continues to tell his own and others' stories from the past.

He and his wife Cherie now live in a farmhouse on five acres near Snohomish, Washington. Four of their five children live nearby and one daughter resides in Leadville.

This is his first book.

"I am so pleased to see the tremendous work that Doug Rhoades has undertaken in his quest to uncover the history of early American food packaging. His discovery of a cache of well preserved early tins, opens up a window into the history of daily life for the miners of the nineteenth century. Those interested in the history of early labeling will find this book of interest."
Dr. Lorne Hammond, Curator of History, Royal B. C. Museum, Victoria, B. C., Canada.

LABELS, LEADVILLE AND LORE

Author (right) with appraiser Rudy Franchi at the Seattle Antiques Roadshow in 2002.

Photo By: Jeff Dunn for WGBH/Boston

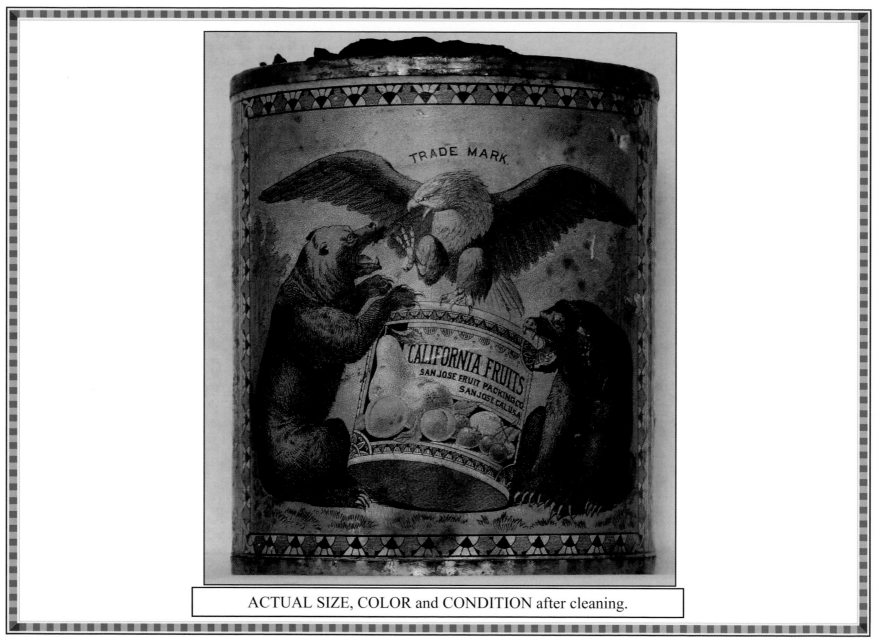

ACTUAL SIZE, COLOR and CONDITION after cleaning.

TABLE OF CONTENTS

RECOMMENDED BOOKS

THE MINING CAMPS SPEAK by Beth and Bill Sagstetter

LEADVILLE'S ICE PALACE by Darlene Godat Weir

THE LABEL MADE ME BUY IT by Ralph and Terry Kovel

REASON FOR WRITING THIS BOOK

In the late 1990's the accidental finding of some seventy old food cans in Leadville, Colorado, most still wrapped in their original labels, began a search to know how rare such items really are. The more people we talked to, along with the research we were doing, indicated they are even more rare than we had at first thought. After buying and studying all the books we could find on labels and early advertising it became apparent that there were not that many of the earliest food can labels saved. No one had seen any of the ones we had found.

Being fans of the Antiques Roadshow, we thought if we could get the cans to the show maybe we could learn more about them. We didn't make it to the Denver show, but after moving to the Seattle area we were able to get tickets to the Seattle show in 2002. At the filming of the cans it was further confirmed we did indeed have a rare, beautiful and unusual collection. The most common expression heard from everyone who saw the cans was: "I've never seen anything like this!"

Once in a while a can or two will be discovered inside a wall, or other out of the way place, but usually without any accompanying history.

One night I was watching and listening with anticipation the Kovel's show about antiques as Mr. Kovel was being interviewed about his tin can label collection. Upon being asked which one was the oldest, he held up a can for mutton from the Range Canning Co., of Ft. McKavett, Texas, and said it was from about 1890. For me those words were thrilling!

These cans with their labels, we now had in our possession, were dated from 1876, and possibly older. This further confirmed we did indeed have a special treasure.

I had heard that the Royal British Columbia Museum in Victoria had some old cans. One of their displays was an old salmon cannery with two old labeled salmon cans. During a tour of their archives I was able to see a scrapbook of salmon labels possibly dating from the 1880's. No dates were included in the scrapbook. At this visit I was encouraged by Dr. Robert Griffin and Dr. Lorne Hammond to write a book about the labels I had found and their history before it's gone. This reinforced my own thoughts and those of my brother-in-law, Dick Clark (not the American Bandstand one), who has been telling me since we found them: "You've got a book in those cans!" With the labels on the cans as a reference, a wealth of history was found that further made it imperative to record what we could before the physical evidence was gone. In all normal conditions these labels would already be gone.

After the book was begun I made a trip to Leadville in October of 2004. Following up on a story I heard after arriving, I was allowed by an agreeable homeowner to look under one of his structures to see if any cans with labels, that had been seen in the 1970's, were still there. Most of the cans had been cleaned out years earlier and apparently discarded permanently, however some cans still remained. I was able to recover a number of cans from the early 1890's and some still had readable labels.

The poor condition of this second cache of labeled cans in a somewhat protected environment further emphasized the rarity of the 1882 and earlier labels. The second cache of cans and their history are also included in the following pages.

INTRODUCTION

Picking up interesting and colorful objects has proven irresistible for millions of individuals. Whenever we are strolling on a beach, finding seashells, driftwood and pretty stones, with the thought of finding a gold coin, we pick things up. At any age when walking in the mountains, plains or deserts, our eyes scan the ground for any object that catches our fancy. Rare is the time we would come home without something in our pocket. At the present time in many areas laws have been passed to protect certain artifacts. Certainly if not for the collector of the past and present much of human history would have been lost forever. Archeologists and historians can only find and research so much with their limited time and resources, and time and certain artifacts wait for no one.

This book is a pictorial and written history of interesting and beautiful objects (primarily the cans), and how they were found. Most of these things had been discarded or lost and forgotten. Others are collections that began with a found 'treasure' and added to over the years.

Entire books have been written on folklore. The lore included here was either found with the cans, or gives additional information that is not common knowledge, but is certainly interesting as to how it ties into the story of the cans and their labels.

In the process of remodeling and restoring older homes it is not unusual to find lost or discarded things.

Our first serious remodeling began in 1972 in Salem, Oregon, with the purchase of a home built in 1910. It continued for over 25 years, ending in Leadville, Colorado, in a home originally constructed in 1878.

During these years of remodeling I would haul things home that most people would haul to the dump, which in past years was itself a treasure trove of discarded history. Today people aren't usually allowed to salvage, so now if you throw history away it is gone.

Our most wonderful treasure trove of discarded history are the cans with their labels found under a house in Leadville. Leadville history helps explain why the cans were there and why they survived. The time period is important because all of the historical happenings of that particular time and place led to this small segment of history being preserved in possibly the only place it could have been.

In an effort to learn more about the labels, additional history was uncovered. Old photos, from libraries and personal collections, help us visualize what life was like then and why this rare piece of history survived in this particular town.

Early American Artifacts

HOW THE FIRST LABELED CANS
WERE FOUND

In the process of replacing a wooden foundation with one of concrete, it was necessary to crawl under the house to repair some damage. Somewhere near the middle, an object was reflecting the beam from my flashlight. This house was so close to the ground I had to tunnel under a log beam and squeeze through to see what was shining back at me. It was a nearly bare shiny tin can. Upon further investigation there proved to be two piles of empty old discarded tin cans. Most contractors just leave whatever trash is under a house right where it lays, but I have always had some need to clean it up. I began tossing the cans over to the side where my son Kelly could reach them and load them in the truck. His first comment was: "Did you see the date on this can?" I answered him that I hadn't. He said: "It's August 7th, 1877!" I now began the slow process of one by one placing each can on top of the log beam, crawling back under it and carrying the cans to the side of the house. By the time we were finished we had an accumulation of over 70 cans, with at least 50 still having a complete or partial label.

We also found a pickle bottle, two beer bottles, three inkwells, parts of five different newspapers, a business card, an old felt hat and what appears to be an advertising brochure for a brothel.

Some of the items found

The reason these cans still had their labels was not just the dry climate at the altitude of 10,200 ft. and the lack of paper eating bugs, it was because the cans were laying on from two to four inches of wood chips. These chips had kept the cans dry. If not for a mouse making a nest out of chewed up labels in one of the bean cans, nearly all of the labels would have been intact.

The original house was constructed of logs that were hewn out at the home site. All the wood chips along with the 'leftovers' from the construction workers lunchtime were tossed to the center of the structure during the time they were building the exterior walls and the roof. The workers installed the floor last because it was the only finished lumber. Once the roof was on, the floor would not get wet and warp. With the floor installed the debris remained nearly undisturbed for over 115 years. You could see parts of a few cans that missed the chips and they were rusted remnants. An extensive study of all the artifacts indicates that most of the cans were opened and the contents eaten in July of 1882.

The early years of canned food labeling is all but missing in history books, probably due to the fact that no one intentionally saved a bean can. Also canneries opened and closed quite rapidly. This accidental discovery led to the opportunity to save an important piece of otherwise forgotten history. These can labels are so beautiful in their art and graphics that they needed to be shared. May you enjoy this book as much as we did putting it together.

EARLY HISTORY OF CANNED FOODS

Past generations have required that most of an individuals waking hours be spent in a quest for each days food. Vast areas of the earth today haven't changed that much. What has changed the way we are able to live today, as much as anything, is our knowledge of preserving food.

A short history of the preserving of food, besides the drying, pickling, salting or fermenting of it, builds an appreciation for the tin can and the label wrapped around it.

In mankind's history, war seems to accelerate the need for new inventions. In the 1790's Napoleon had discovered that more of his men were dying from poor diet or spoiled food than in battle. In 1795 the French government began **The Society for Encouragement of New Inventions.** To encourage someone to find a way to preserve food to feed the French armies, a reward of 12,000 francs was offered to whoever invented a process. Nicolas Appert collected the 12,000 francs in 1809 by stuffing small bits of food into champagne bottles, heating them sufficiently, and sealing them with a cork and sealing wax. Tin containers were patented in England in 1810. Now opposing armies had a supply of preserved food.

The first fruit orchards of California, besides those around the eighteenth-century Missions, began to produce fruit in 1850. These first small orchards soon became invaluable with the masses of people flocking to California because of the 'gold rush.' At this time in history the number of these orchards were recorded as a 'dozen' or so, certainly not enough to supply the needs of the expanding population.

Whenever there is a need it doesn't take long for someone to step up to fill that need. The year, 1854, saw Daniel R. Provost arrive at San Francisco as a representative of Wells, Provost & Co. of Yonkers, N.Y., packers of bottled fruits, jams, jellies and pickles. Generally these were shipped around the Horn on clipper ships in firkins (small wooden casks), then repacked into small glass containers to be sold. By 1856 Provost was making his own preserves and jellies from native fruit, but still using nothing but glass containers. This marked the beginning of West Coast packing.

In November of 1857 Francis Cutting arrived in San Francisco from Massachusetts. By June of 1858 he was in business packing preserves, fruits and jellies in glass jars. In the spring of 1860 Cutting received a large shipment of Mason fruit jars, which had been patented in 1858. These jars were used until 1862, when the first tin plate was brought around the horn, made into tin cans, filled and shipped back around the horn to supply the needs created by the Civil War.

1858 Mason jars

That year Cutting canned 5,400 cases of California fruits. By 1865 his output had increased to 12,500 cases, many of the cans being two-gallon, two-and-one-half gallon and five gallon 'tins.'

By 1937 there were 40,000 manufacturing establishments pasting little labels on eight billion tin cans per year. In 2004 the number was two-hundred billion.

Some of the old labels have little to say, but others give very lengthy information and directions for use. This early information and the graphics are so interesting that we have included different views, and most of the writing from the cans that is identifiable.

Whenever information is quoted from a label, in most cases it is done in bold letters in a proportion similar to how it appears on the label.

These are five old **1858 MASON** jars with zinc lids. The larger one on the left is two quarts, the one on the right is one quart and the three at the bottom right are one pint. They are called 'Midgets.' They have their own special smaller size lid. All three are a little different in size, and are embossed differently. Two have **PAT. NOV. 26, 67,** embossed on the bottom. The one in the middle has **C. F. J. Co**. embossed on the back; the initials of the Consolidated Fruit Jar Co. of New York. This company registered the trademark word **MASON** on Oct. 28, 1879. Each has a different number. The rims on the jars have all been ground to make a seal possible. It was not until around 1900 that other kinds of bottles and jars started to change from corks and glass stoppers to the screw lid.

Please do not consider this book an authority on glass jars or bottles.

This label is from the oldest packing company on the West coast.

The representation of a griffin was first used in 1858 by the **Cutting Packing Co.**

This trademark of a **GRIFFIN** was used for 32 years before it was registered in 1890.

The griffin was a mythical half lion, half eagle.

This blackberry can label was a victim of the mouse mentioned previously.

The side that is missing was a view of San Francisco, and the Bay.

The printer was the
SCHMIDT LABEL & LITH. CO. S. F.

The blue and white label for Eagle Brand Condensed Milk was used from 1857 until the 1920's. These are well remembered because of the full page advertising pictures in magazines and signs that are collected today.

A can of Ezra A. Edgett's "Green Corn" of 1865 bore a black and white label, and when opened in 1916 at Harvard University was proven to be safely edible. Burnham & Morrill's Paris Brand Oat Meal, awarded a gold medal at the Paris Exposition of 1878, wore a black and white label in the 1880's.

The first mention of more than two colors on a label that I have found was trademark #1967 of September 8, 1874. It was for Canned Salmon by Cutting and Co. of San Francisco, Calif. The trademark reads as follows: 'A semi-circular picture of a Salmon on the hither shore. Water in middle distance and mountains across the background, the whole printed in colors.'

Fewer than fifty American families can trace their ancestors' canning activities back to the 1870's, which tells us that there were not many different labels from those early dates. No one knows when the first colored label was put on a tin can, however this much is known:

During the 1850's Nathan Winslow was selling Winslow's Patent Hermetically Sealed Corn of Maine under a well-known yellow label of that time.

This is an early can that was completely wrapped with paper before the label was pasted on.

Several cans like this one were found that still had the label attached so we know this one contained corn from Maine.

The cleaner area reveals where the label was.

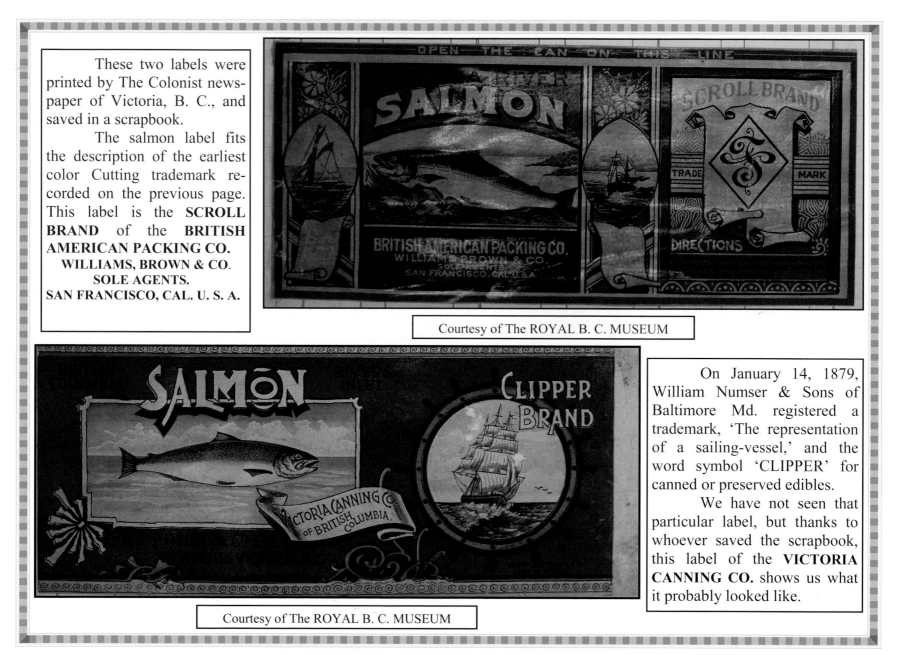

These two labels were printed by The Colonist newspaper of Victoria, B. C., and saved in a scrapbook.

The salmon label fits the description of the earliest color Cutting trademark recorded on the previous page. This label is the **SCROLL BRAND** of the **BRITISH AMERICAN PACKING CO.**
WILLIAMS, BROWN & CO.
SOLE AGENTS.
SAN FRANCISCO, CAL. U. S. A.

Courtesy of The ROYAL B. C. MUSEUM

On January 14, 1879, William Numser & Sons of Baltimore Md. registered a trademark, 'The representation of a sailing-vessel,' and the word symbol 'CLIPPER' for canned or preserved edibles.

We have not seen that particular label, but thanks to whoever saved the scrapbook, this label of the **VICTORIA CANNING CO.** shows us what it probably looked like.

Courtesy of The ROYAL B. C. MUSEUM

These are two more of the early labels printed by the Victoria, B. C. newspaper. During their off hours, many newspapers in their early years printed a wide variety of labels, business cards and fliers.

The **DIRECTIONS** on these labels were all similar. 'To serve hot, place can before being opened in boiling water for thirty minutes. Empty as soon as opened.'

The warning to empty the contents immediately was based on the erroneous thought that once air got to the food it would react with the can and be harmful to your health.

In reality it would spoil at the same rate in the opened can as in any other container. Certain foods would absorb a metallic taste if left in older cans.

THE CAN THAT WAS NEARLY OVERLOOKED

A few weeks prior to the 'big' discovery a small can fell out from under the house while we were digging along the first side. I thought it interesting enough to haul home and place it on a shelf in the barn because it was a 'cute' little can. It had a partial label that I recognized so I didn't think of it as being especially old.

In the excitement of trying to find out how rare the 'big find' was, I didn't even think about the first can. Some months later while looking for some misplaced tool I noticed the can. Picking it up I observed the hand soldered side and then knew it was as old as the others.

From the standpoint of history this can is one of the most exciting. To my knowledge it is the only original Red Devil on an original can in existence. The trademark was first used in 1867 or 1868 and is the oldest registered food trademark still in use in the U. S. today. The little devil has been redrawn four times. The survival of the Underwood can was not because of the wood chips. The can itself had been coated with some kind of lacquer that gave the can a greenish hue. The label was applied after this process.

Over 115 years in the dry dirt took its toll, but left enough for us to identify what it was.

A little history about William Underwood makes this can still more exciting. He arrived in Boston from London in 1819, by way of New Orleans. By 1826 he was supplying customers from Boston to Buenos Aires with preserved fruits and vegetables. In 1839 he changed from glass bottles and jars to tin containers. A major reason for this change was because glass was breaking during shipping. Before this time there were no 'tin cans.'

When Peter Durand received a patent for a 'tin plated sheet steel container for food,' it was called a 'tin canister.' This was before 1817.

Sometime between 1839 and 1849, Underwood bookkeepers shortened 'canister' to 'can,' and a new word was added to the English language.

An interesting report, in a Boston newspaper from 1849 was that the first gold to reach Boston from California was brought across the continent in an otherwise empty Underwood tin can.

Because the Red Devil is the oldest registered food trademark in use today, although revised four times, now would be an appropriate time to give a little history concerning trademarks.

TRADEMARK HISTORY

The first federal law on the subject was not passed until 1870, and the first TRADEMARK was registered on July 8, 1870. It was registered by the Averill Chemical Paint Company and was represented by an eagle holding in its beak a pot of paint and a pennant with a slogan.

Knowing this history explains why a trademark used since 1868 was not filed until Oct 25, 1870. There was not yet an office to file it in.

Unlike patents and copyrights, trademarks are not mentioned in the Constitution.

After nine years of uninterrupted registration the Supreme Court in 1879 declared the Trademark Law of 1870 unconstitutional.

Whoever was in charge of registering the trademarks continued to do so although there was no legal reason for doing it. This continued through February of 1881. From March 8, 1881, until May 18, 1881, no trademarks were registered. This was evidently because new laws were being enacted. These new laws again allowed for trademarks to be registered, but not for interstate commerce, making the trademark laws nearly meaningless.

On May 19, 1881, they were once again registering trademarks, and this continued until 1905. New Trademark Laws were then enacted that now included interstate, foreign and native tribes of this country. These are still the basic laws that govern trademarks in the U. S. A. today. At this time the companies still in business began re-registering their trademarks, including Underwood's 'Deviled Ham.'

Because of the legalities involved with the United States Trademark Laws, Great Britain claims the first and oldest legal trademark, having opened their **Department of Registration of Trademarks** in London on January 1, 1876. The first registered trademark was the red triangle of the company 'Bass & Co,' which they used on bottles of ale.

Closely related to the registering of trademarks was the registering of labels. This began on August 1, 1874, with the first registered label going to The Pearl Hominy Co. of Baltimore. The title was 'Breakfast Hominy.'

The reason trademarks are given so much attention in this book is because nearly all of the labels we found had trademarks and this was the best way to confirm their age. During the research of trademarks, the history they revealed was fascinating. If the history tied in with the early canning and labeling industry we have included it.

The trademark is recorded as the following:
'The pictorial group, consisting of the American
eagle, with spread wings, surmounting a large can or
package, two grizzly bears and California fruit, all substantially as illustrated and described.'

The artwork in the graphics on this label is outstanding, even the look in the eye of the eagle tells a story. The entire label is so beautiful it's surprising they threw the can away.

The San Jose Fruit Packing Co. got its start in 1873 by Dr. J. M. Dawson and his son, T. B. Dawson.

The grizzly would have been a fitting subject to grab your attention at this time in California history. It is found on the seal and flag of the State of California.

The following story recorded in a newspaper, discovered on a wall of our home during renovations, adds to the grizzlies part in the lore of the West.

**From THE HERALD DEMOCRAT:
LEADVILLE, SUNDAY, September 15, 1895.
NO TALKING WANTED
When the Old Man Killed a Bear, He
Liked Things Quiet.**

"Bear?" Said Mr. Ottinger. "Bear? Why, I helped to kill a 1,140 pound grizzly once at Wawona. Old Jim Duncan, the slayer of 94 bears, and I went out on horseback about ten miles from town after grouse. We walked five or six miles in the hottest weather, and after getting six grouse and a hundred mosquitoes we thought of turning back home. I was so thirsty that I said, 'Wait for me at the clearing, Jim, till I go down the canyon to get a drink.' I went down about 200 feet and had to lie sprawling over rocks in order to drink. I only took one swallow when two gunshots rang out. Startled at the sound I rose up and ran as well as my weight would let me back to the clearing. Puffing and blowing I leaned up against a tree and witnessed the strangest sight that I ever saw. A big pile of fur lay in a heap on the ground, and the old hunter was just about to jab his bowie knife into it when the bundle rose up like a flash and let out a blow that sent Jim's musket spinning 50 feet in the air. With that there was the most exciting fight that I ever saw. "The bear reared up again and Duncan barely dodged its claws, but bruin caught his clothes at the neck and ripped them down to his boots. I still leaned against the tree, too weary from my run and too surprised to get up and shoot the bear. I could see Duncan slip around and his feet got tangled in his torn clothes. He fell fighting with the bear atop, but the bear's throat was cut from ear to ear. The old man extracted himself and sliding on the carcass called over to me through his nose: 'Waal, my time hasn't come yet. Young man, I give you credit for a great deal of coolness for a greenhorn. I'm glad you didn't open your mouth in this fracas. So many of these fellows think they have to talk when I'm killing a b'ar.'"   San Francisco, Call.*

*as written in the paper

A part of the piece of newspaper with the story.

16

About 20 miles E.N.E of Mariposa we located the little town of Wawona, on the edge of Yosemite National Park. Ten miles from Wawona was the location of the bear story found in the 1895 newspaper article recorded on the proceeding page. The **WAWONA** is also the name of an 1890's wooden sailing vessel being restored in the Seattle area.

This label is mostly gone, but what remains is very unique in that it could be used in two ways. This can was identified as **TABLE FRUITS**, but if the label was overlapped the other way it could be used for **PIE FRUIT.**

What is left of the picture further emphasizes that getting consumers attention was important. Besides the fancy graphics there appears to be a Roman with a helmet and a red garment over his shoulder flapping in the wind (my imagination pictures him in a chariot), and there is a little owl in the background. It seems that the artist drew whatever they personally liked into the design.

The Little Owl

The only **MARIPOSA** we could find is a town and county east of Merced, California.
Looking for Mariposa on the California map led to another example of tying history together.

17

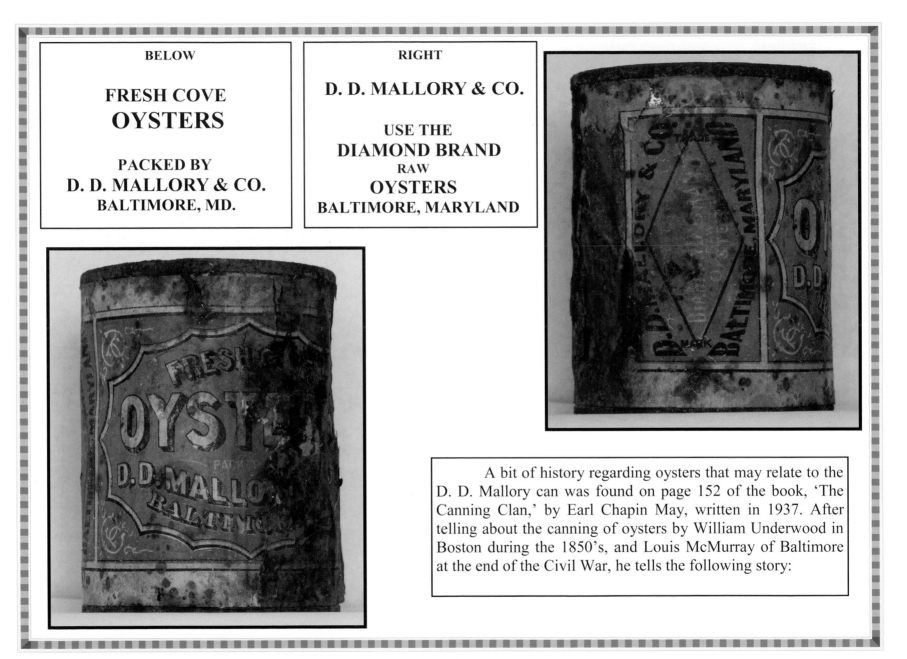

BELOW

FRESH COVE
OYSTERS

PACKED BY
D. D. MALLORY & CO.
BALTIMORE, MD.

RIGHT

D. D. MALLORY & CO.

USE THE
DIAMOND BRAND
RAW
OYSTERS
BALTIMORE, MARYLAND

A bit of history regarding oysters that may relate to the D. D. Mallory can was found on page 152 of the book, 'The Canning Clan,' by Earl Chapin May, written in 1937. After telling about the canning of oysters by William Underwood in Boston during the 1850's, and Louis McMurray of Baltimore at the end of the Civil War, he tells the following story:

"Another canner, whose name has been lost, made 'Baltimore' oysters and cove oysters almost synonymous when he added 'Cove' to a brand of bivalves. Millions of purchasers of these 'Cove' oysters assumed that they came from coves or inlets of Chesapeake Bay. That is not the way 'Cove' originated. Two 'oyster shops' were located opposite each other on a small street or alley, which Baltimore of 1870 knew as 'Cove Street.' One shop dealt exclusively in 'raw' or 'fresh' oysters. The other shop sold only bivalves which had been processed and sealed hermetically in cans. The dealer in 'raws' objected when the competitor labeled his containers 'Fresh Chesapeake Oysters.' To differentiate between raw and cooked oysters the other dealer announced that his were 'Cove Oysters.' In a short time 'Cove' came to mean almost any Baltimore oyster."

The Baltimore fire of 1904 wiped out 'Cove Street' along with their names and places. It is very possible that the other canner was D. D. Mallory, especially since he registered his trademark on Sept.10, 1872. What we do know is that his history survived on a can under a house in Colorado.

This common product is quite uncommon in that it survived being thrown away, buried and dug back up without being broken. What is even more unusual is that it is etched on the glass at its base, **LEADVILLE**. You can make out the **LE** one quarter inch down from the metal base. Only two letters can be seen at a time as the bulb is rotated.

This antique fishing reel fell out of an attic area as I was removing a soffit board that needed to be replaced. It got my attention by hitting me on the head. Any remodeling of an older home can uncover lost or discarded treasures behind or under any wall or board.

This is the best example of the oldest Borden's label known to exist.

Five tin cans that had contained Borden's condensed milk were found. The amount of information on these small cans is astonishing.

This information is printed below and on the next two pages so you don't have to try to read it off of the label.

Trade Mark of the NEW YORK CONDENSED MILK CO.

GAIL BORDEN
EAGLE   BRAND
By which their PRESERVED MILK will hereafter be designated; and for additional protection against imposition, each label will bear the signature,

Gail Borden

OFFICE NEW YORK CONDENSED MILK CO.
79 Murray Street, New York.

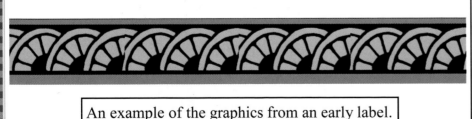

An example of the graphics from an early label.

NEXT PAGE—

CONDENSED MILK
THE GAIL BORDEN
EAGLE BRAND
CONDENSED BY THE
NEW YORK CONDENSED MILK COMPANY

By Process Patented by GAIL BORDEN
This PRESERVED MILK is Condensed Milk, combined with best Refined Sugar, and is the same article as that sold for seven years prior to 1866 by the New York Condensed Milk Co. as
BORDEN'S CONDENSED MILK;
but other manufactures of inferior qualities having appropriated to themselves our original brand, the New York Condensed Milk Co. found it expedient in January 1866, to adopt another brand, viz... the "EAGLE BRAND." (Registered)

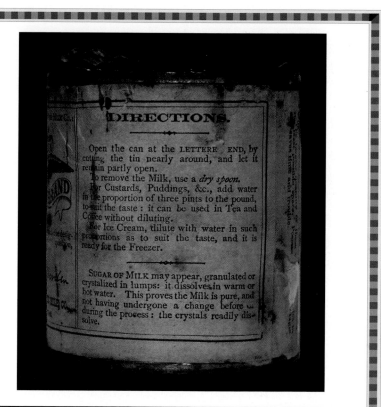

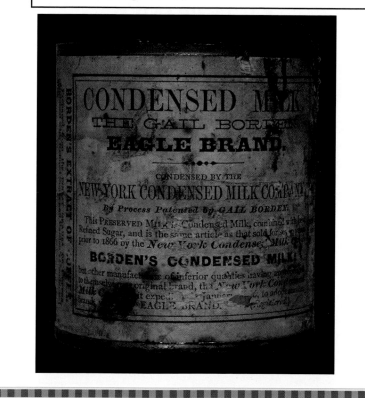

DIRECTIONS

Open the can at the LETTERED END, by cutting the tin nearly around, and let it remain partly open.
To remove the milk, use a *dry spoon*. For Custards, Puddings, &c., add water in the proportion of three pints to the pound, to suit the taste: it can be used in Tea and Coffee without diluting.
For Ice Cream, dilute with water in such proportions as to suit the taste, and it is ready for the freezer.

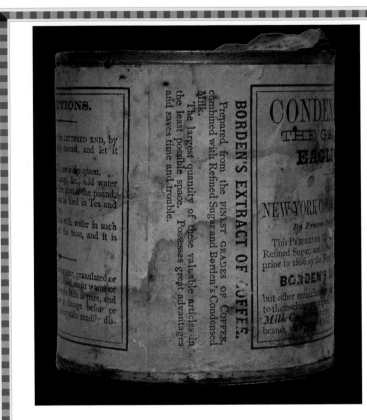

BORDEN'S EXTRACT OF COFFEE

Prepared from the FINEST GRADES OF COFFEE, combined with Refined Sugar and Borden's Condensed Milk.

The largest quantity of these valuable articles in the least possible space. Possesses great advantages and saves time and trouble.

Engraved on the top:
EAGLE BRAND
NEW YORK CONDENSED MILK CO.

(Continued from previous page)

Sugar of Milk may appear, granulated or crystal-lized in lumps: it dissolves in warm or hot water. This proves the Milk is pure, and not having undergone a change before or during the process: the crystals readily dissolve.

An empty tin can is able to give us some insight on individuals from the past. Upon closer examination of the Borden cans we noticed that four out of five of those who opened the cans had followed the directions and opened them on the right end. Further examination revealed that two of the cans had been signed in solder with the letters CO.

The CO on the bottom of the can.

One has just the letter O. Another was too rusted to tell, and the last one has a tiny stamped o. The letters could have identified the work of the tin smith to get paid, a mark to tell which batch of cans it was for quality evaluation, or in the fashion of early craftsman he chose to sign his work.

The O on the bottom of the can.

This is a full page magazine advertisement, with the copyright of 1911, by Borden's Condensed Milk Co. This is an example of advertising from that time period that proved very effective then, and has a strong appeal today. Collectors value this early artwork because of the baby, the majesty of the eagle, and even the history of the label and can.

The can held by the eagle is an example of the hole-and-cap cans that were being phased out by the machine pressed on lids. This label is very similar to the earlier ones we found except the address is different. The embossing on the top reads **BORDEN'S CONDENSED MILK CO.** instead of **NEW YORK CONDENSED MILK CO.**

The circular piece of metal found in one of the second batch of cans tells us a story.

This round cap appears to have been cut out by a machine. We know it was never fully attached because no pinhole, soldered shut, is in the middle.

Whoever was soldering the cap over the hole dropped this cap inside the can after starting to solder it in place. Instead of pulling it out he soldered another cap in place, leaving the extra cap in with the food.

The consumer who emptied the contents either didn't notice the extra lid or didn't care.

BORDEN'S EAGLE BRAND CONDENSED MILK
Has protected Babies from Summer Ills for 54 Years.
Send for Baby's Book "My Biography"
BORDEN'S CONDENSED MILK CO., NEW YORK.
"Leaders of Quality" — Est. 1857.

Although the eagle is still on Borden's labels, it has diminished in recognition by the appearance of Elsie the cow in 1939. This paper advertising sign hanging on a wall at The Rivers Edge Cafe in Snohomish, Washington., is pre-1939.

The older Borden's cans did not indicate what their weight was. By their size we know they contained 10 ounces. This later label reports a net weight of 14 1/2 ounces and 13 ounces liquid measure.

Our friend Morris Gay, born in Leadville in 1922, whose family owned a dairy, remembers how boys growing up during the depression would stomp on these taller milk cans until they curled around their hard soled shoes. You could then make all kinds of neat noise running on a hard surface. Morris also remembered that he had to get rid of them before he got home or he was in trouble. The cans would tear up the sides of the shoes.

I remember doing the same thing in the early 50's, but I had forgotten that they tore up your shoes.

A milk related collectable advertising item.
This spoon was advertising PET MILK.

25

HIGHLAND BRAND
TRADE   MARK

CONDENSED MILK
**Prepared by Patented
Process by the**
HELVETIA MILK CONDENS'G CO.
Highland, Ills.

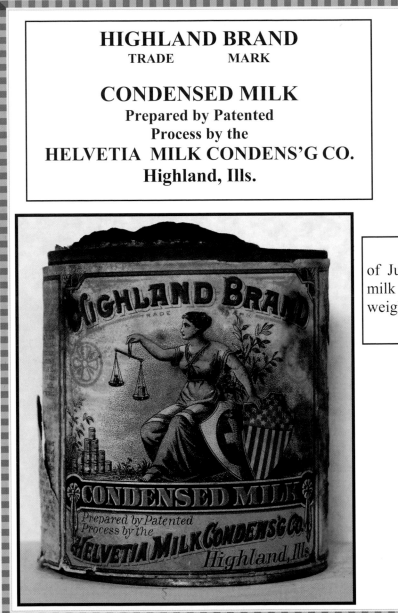

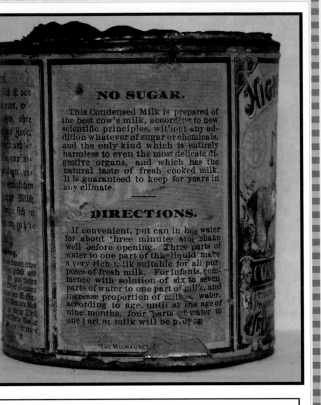

In the scales of Justice there is a milk can tipping the weight in its favor.

NO SUGAR.

This Condensed Milk is prepared of the best cow's milk, according to new scientific principles, without any addition whatever of sugar or chemicals, and the only kind which is entirely harmless to even the most delicate digestive organs, and which has the natural taste of fresh cooked milk. It is guaranteed to keep for years in any climate.

It was printed by **THE MILWAUKEE LITHO.& ENGR. CO.**

DIRECTIONS.

If convenient, put can in hot water for three minutes and shake well before opening. Three parts of water to one part of this liquid make a very rich milk suitable for all purposes of fresh milk. For infants, commence with solution of six to seven parts of water to one part of milk, and increase proportion of milk to water according to age, until at the age of nine months, four parts of water to one part of milk will be proper.

The information and directions were printed in three languages.

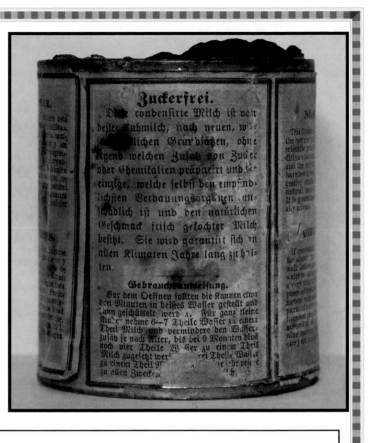

German

Spanish

The Highland Brand was the first company to can milk without sugar. The experimental process had its beginnings in Switzerland by John B. Meyenberg in 1881 while working at the Anglo-Swiss Condensed Milk Company. They weren't interested in his experiments at that time. He then came to America and patented his process on November 25, 1884. By 1885 he was shipping some of his first efforts to the mining camps of the West. This can ended up near the others when someone cut a hole in the floor to construct a brick chimney. This is the Helvetia Company's first design. They modernized their design in the 1890's, and simplified Lady Justice.

Her shields were changed from the emblems of the United States and Switzerland to one shield of red, white and black and the other shield having the letters 'H. M. Co.' The later design has the date 1893 on it.

above

This can was located and purchased from an antique mall in Snohomish, Washington.

The Helvetia Company sold their product mainly in the South and West under different brand names. The most popular brand was **PET,** registered in 1895. The results of a dairymen strike in 1920 forced the closure of the Highland plant. In 1921 they were located in St. Louis. Two years later they changed their name to the 'Pet Milk Company.' This knowledge dates this can's age between 1921 and 1923. Their name on this label was still Helvetia, but they were now located in St. Louis.

These two milk pitchers were perhaps premiums that were obtained by sending in labels from Pet Milk. The larger one holds two and a half cups, and the smaller one holds one and a half cups.

The variety of canned goods being shipped into this boom town was not limited to the borders of the United States. This sardine can imported from Paris, France, was found with the others. **PARIS** is embossed on the top. This was the only one of the earlier cans with the label printed directly onto the metal. The darker areas on the can are for the most part olive oil. It helped the can survive with very little rust.

The interior of the can is coated with the oil. The lack of decomposing bacteria at this altitude preserved the oil and the can.

Paris was the sardine capital of the world in the 1880's.

Each side of the can is printed in a different language, English, German, French, and Spanish.

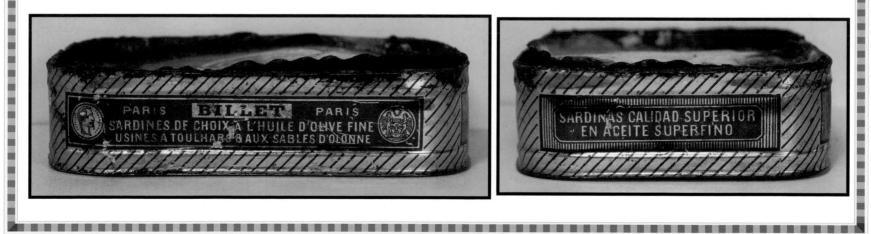

29

COMPRESSED   COOKED
CORNED BEEF
Libby, McNeill & Libby
CHICAGO

This can was discovered at an antique shop in Halifax, Nova Scotia one week before Halifax was struck by a hurricane in the fall of 2003. It may be older than 1880.

The label is after 1878 and before 1884.

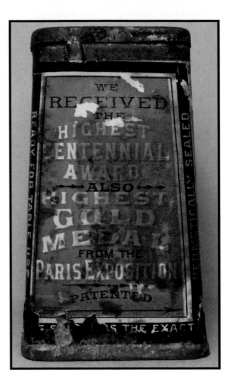

I mention the hurricane because while researching the history of the labels I came across the history of the fires and natural disasters that destroyed so much of the early cities and towns. It makes it even more remarkable that labels like these survived at all.

The narrow end of the label above tells us:

WE	-ALSO-
RECEIVED	**HIGHEST**
THE	**GOLD MEDAL**
HIGHEST	FROM THE
CENTENNIAL	**PARIS EXPOSITION**
AWARD	PATENTED

These two events were in 1876 and 1878.

The oldest Libby, McNeill & Libby label we had seen before this one reads:
Libby, McNeill & Libby
RECEIVED THE ONLY
GOLD & SILVER
MEDALS
AWARDED BY THE
INTERNATIONAL
HEALTH EXHIBITION
LONDON 1884
GOLD MEDAL
PARIS EXPOSITION
HIGHEST AWARD
WORLD'S COLUMBIAN
EXPOSTION, CHICAGO
This would date it after 1892.

Above is the other end of the can.

The inside of this can is an example of the earlier work of using too much solder. Later Libby, McNeill & Libby did, over a period of years, save more than $1,000,000 in the cost of lead by learning how to use less solder, and they finally eliminated its use.

You may draw your own conclusions as to the effects on health.

The top is embossed
L. Mc. & L.
CHICAGO.
The corners of the label are printed:
WARRANTED TO KEEP IN ALL CLIMATES
BONELESS AND ECONOMICAL
READY FOR TABLE USE
HERMETICALLY SEALED
The wording around the bottom is missing about 25% of its message.
The part that can be read is:
----NCE OPENING THIS CAN USE AN
ORDINARY CAN OPENER, FOLLOW
LOWER EDGE OF CAN AROUND
THE SIDES THE EXACT—

It looks as if a can opener was used.

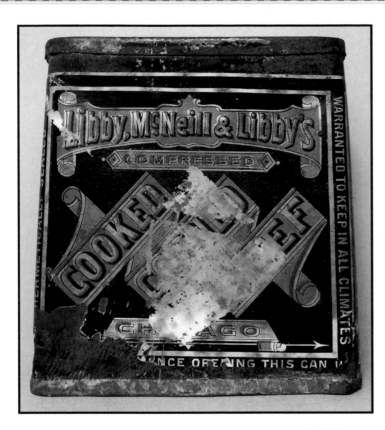

On the back of the can it reads:

Libby, McNeill & Libby's
COMPRESSED
COOKED CORNED BEEF
CHICAGO

Libby, McNeill & Libby started canning corned beef in Chicago in straight sided cans that cost ten cents a-piece in 1868.

They discovered, after a long search at the patent office in Washington D.C., a dormant patent of a Mr. Marshall from 1864. It was for a device that squeezed excess water and air out of corned beef, molded and shaped it to fit the container. They paid Mr. Marshall $75 to assign them his patent. The Wilson Packing Co. had a patent for a plunger that would press the meat into a slightly tapered can with rounded corners. They now needed a tapered can.

They pooled their resources and began producing tapered cans. They employed a North Side can-maker and in 1875 began using the tapered can.

These were more complicated than the cylindrical cans and it took many years to perfect them.

When other canneries started using the tapered can, Libby, McNeill & Libby spent $250,000 defending their patent only to have the United States Supreme Court rule that the tapered can could not be patented because the old cake pans, used by almost every cook and housewife in the country, had the same features.

The tapered can is still in use today.

These pictures are of a miniature for a child's kitchen. The photos show the can at its actual size. As much information was on this little can as on the full sized one.

The front and back are nearly identical to the actual label. The biggest difference is there are no directions on how to open the can since it was only a toy.

COMPRESSED COOKED
CORNED BEEF
PACKED BY
Libby, McNeill & Libby

WE RECEIVED THE

HIGHEST AWARDS
AT THE
INTERNATIONAL
HEALTH EXPOSITION
LONDON, 1884
PARIS EXPOSITION
WORLD'S COLUMBIAN
EXPOSITION
CHICAGO, 1893
PANAMA-PACIFIC
INTERNATIONAL
EXPOSITION
SAN FRANCISCO, 1915

Libby, McNeill & Libby's

COMPRESSED
**COOKED
CORNED BEEF**

TRADE MARK

ASK YOUR GROCER FOR
OTHER LIBBY'S CANNED
MEATS, VIENNA SAUSAGE,
VEAL LOAF, DRIED BEEF,
GENUINE DEVILED HAM,
GENUINE POTTED CHICKEN,
CORNED BEEF HASH,
CHILE CON CARNE.
PACKED AT
LIBBY'S MODEL KITCHENS

MADE IN U. S. A.

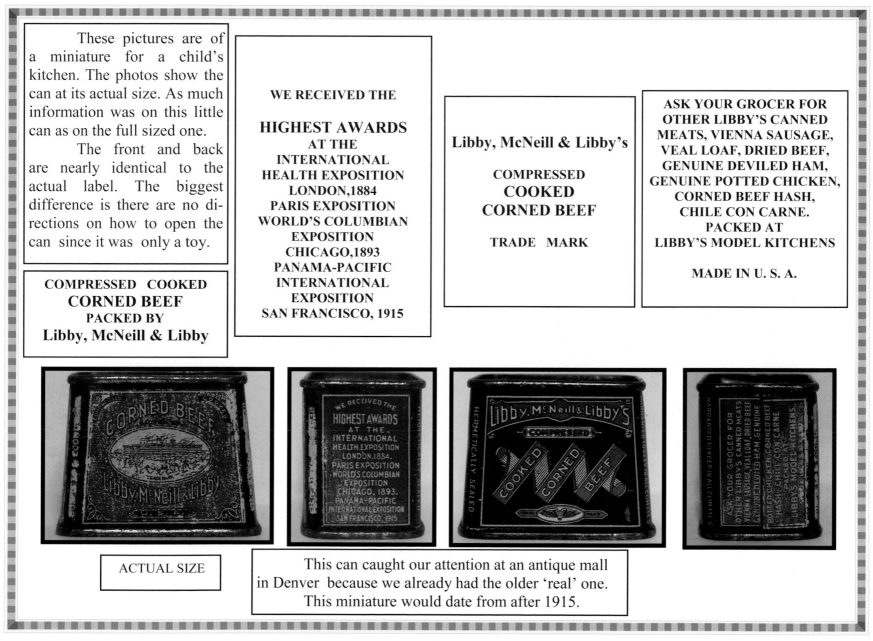

ACTUAL SIZE

This can caught our attention at an antique mall in Denver because we already had the older 'real' one. This miniature would date from after 1915.

33

LOOMIS, ALLEN & Co
SWEET   CORN
TRADE MARK.

CICERO, N. Y.
FORMERLY   SYRACUSE, N. Y.

This label had a trademark but I could not find that it was registered. John Winslow Jones, of Portland, Maine, registered a trademark on May 2, 1876, which reads:

'The combination of a red ground with the representation of an ear of green corn.'

This design appears very similar. 'Green' didn't mean unripe or a color, it was synonymous with sweet, sugar or honey corn.

The printing reading from the bottom up is:
THESE CANS ARE SOLDERED ON THE OUTSIDE.

The small printing in the **DIRECTIONS** box reads: **Open the can on the bottom; empty the corn into a dish suitable for heating it. Heat it thoroughly after adding seasoning, &c. Be careful and not boil the corn, as boiling makes it tough and dark colored.**

The blue scroll at the bottom says:
THIS CORN is picked and packed fresh from the fields, and the consumers will find the Natural Flavor of Green Corn that other brands lack so much.

This label's directions were given in three languages: English, French and German.

The elaborate graphics on this label were beautifully designed to get your attention.

Here we have one of the two different labels that had a paper label on the top of the can that gave directions and other information.

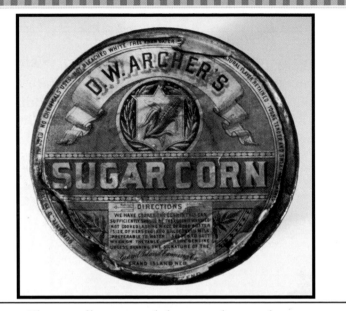

The wording around the top edge reads:

"GUARANTEED (POSTED) $1,000.00 IN GOLD. NO CHEMICALS USED. NOT BLEACHED WHITE. FREE FROM WATER. FREE FROM SUGAR. NATURAL FLAVOR RETAINED. YOUNG, TENDER AND SWEET AND CANNED IN ITS OWN MILK. OPEN THIS END.

In addition to the **D.W. ARCHER'S SUGAR CORN**, the **DIRECTIONS** are:

WE HAVE COOKED THE CORN IN THIS CAN SUFFICIENTLY. SHOULD BE THOROUGHLY WARMED (NOT COOKED), ADDING PIECE OF GOOD BUTTER (SIZE OF HEN'S EGG) AND GILL OF FRESH MILK. (PREFERABLE TO WATER) SEASON TO SUIT WHEN ON THE TABLE.---NONE GENUINE UNLESS BEARING THE SIGNATURE OF THE

GRAND ISLAND CANNING CO.

GRAND ISLAND, NEB.

D.W. ARCHER'S TROPHY
SUGAR CORN

The D.W. Archer Company had another plant at Chillicothe, Ohio that was in financial trouble in 1883. At this time, the C.E. Sears and Company took over the plant in Ohio.

Since financial problems were encountered in 1883, it helps establish that they were producing products before this date. The D.W. Archer Brand was still registering trademarks in August of 1891.

**HONEY. DROP. SUGAR. CORN
PACKED EXPRESSLY FOR CITY TRADE BY
DAVIS, BAXTER & CO.
PORTLAND, ME.**

H. C. Baxter as a member of **DAVIS, BAXTER** and **Co.** began packing lobsters in 1861.

This is an example of a label being used before it was registered. They registered Canned Corn on March 28, 1882, but not the name '**HONEY DROP**' until 1884.

What was meant by **PACKED EXPRESSLY FOR CITY TRADE**, must have been any city since at least six of their cans made it to Colorado in 1882.

This company's label has a feature none of the others had; that the entire can was first wrapped in paper, then one label was pasted on the front and another pasted on the top.

At least two colors of wrapping paper were used, blue and yellow.

All of these labels are so unique in their striking beauty that extra pictures are needed to see it all.

Labels at this period in their development included a great amount of directions. The following information written here is from the top of the can.

NEW SEED HONEY DROP

This corn is grown from seed selected and improved, with the greatest care and when it reaches the proper stage for picking it is cut from the cob and immediately sealed air tight in its own milk.

First quality–Packed at Winthorp, Kennebec County, Maine, U. S. A.

THE USUAL MODE– thoroughly WARM; (not cook) with the addition of a piece of butter the size of a hen's egg and a gill of water or milk, season to taste.

(Continued from the top of the can)
SEE THAT LABEL BEARS THIS SIGNATURE

Davis Baxter Co.

OPEN ON THIS END.

It appears that this can was opened with a knife, but thankfully the fancy lace edge design was left intact.

E. B. MALLORY & CO. registered the trademark of the 'figure of an Arrow' on November 7, 1876.

This is another example of a picture telling a story of the canning industry. The illustration shows the cannery with its exterior fire exit. Horses with wagons are seen in the foreground, and in the background, sailing ships are seen ready to haul the produce around the world.

The writing on the label reads:
**These goods are packed fresh from
the fields where grown at our own
Packing House.
Galesville, Anne Arundel Co. Md.
E. B. Mallory & Co.
Printed by the National Bureau of Engraving, Philadelphia.**

This label is an exquisite example of the quality of paper used on these early labels. The surface is slick enough that I was able to clean most of them with a Q-tip, mild soap and water.

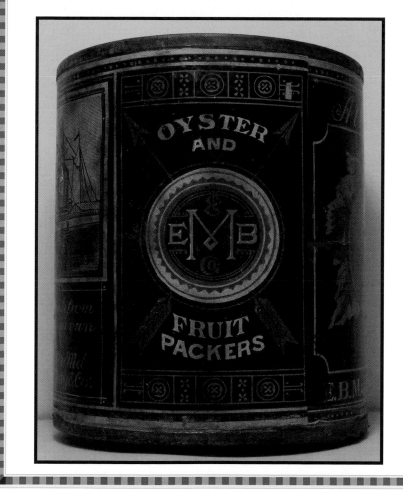

After laying under a house for more than 115 years, this label had held up the best of them all. The actual size of this can is five inches tall by four and a quarter inches across.

Galesville is a town about twenty miles south of Annapolis, Maryland, and according to the 2000 census had a population of 1000.

Louis McMurray was the canning king of Baltimore in the 1880's, and Baltimore was considered the canning capitol of America. In 1888 he was sole owner and manager of the 'Largest Corn Factory in the World'!

Early canning involved a great deal of trial and error. How long you boiled the product and how hot its temperature reached made the difference of making a profit or loosing your entire production.

Around 1860, Isaac Solomon following the earlier experiments of British chemist Sir Humphry Davy, added calcium chloride to the water, thereby raising the temperature from 212 to 240 degrees Fahrenheit. This reduced the boiling time of four to six hours to twenty-five to forty minutes and resulted in less spoilage. Mr. McMurray adopted this process and was able to raise production from 2,500 cans a day to 20,000 cans, just in time for the Civil War.

By the end of the Civil War, food and condensed milk in cans had been accepted as a safe means of obtaining needed nourishment under all circumstances.

Mr. McMurray was resourceful to the extreme. In 1868, upon failure of the Maryland and Delaware peach crop, he packed up all of his equipment and crew and moved them to Cincinnati, where there was an abundance of peaches.

On June 2, 1876, he registered trademarks for the word **MOUNTAIN** for canned or preserved corn, and the representation of a **DEER** for other canned goods. On Jan.1, 1878, for preserved green corn he registered the trademark 'the word and symbol **EAGLE**,' #5,546.

Another trademark #7,815 was issued to Louis McMurray on Feb.10, 1880, for canned oysters. The trademark was 'the letters **I. X. L.**'

Since this label bears no trademark it could be older.

At least one **BLUEBERRY** can survived to help remember Louis McMurray's vast canning empire. He died at the height of his career in 1888.

Just an interesting note regarding trademarks is how little a difference there can be between them. A trademark, re-registered on March 25, 1879, 'for chopping axes' were the fanciful, selected letters **I X L** (without the periods). Louis McMurray's 'for oysters' was **I. X. L.** (with periods).

BURNHAM & MORRILL began their canning history together in 1867, although George Burnham Jr. had been canning Maine products during the 1850's.

B & M is still in business. I was able to find their phone number and called, hoping to hear that they had a museum. I was able to talk to a 'real person' about finding one of their first colored labels. She was very helpful when I talked with her, but she knew of no museum that maintained an in depth history of the canning industry.

This was the beginning of a long quest to find out if any company, in the world of food preserving, has a pictorial history about the first canning labels. To this date I have not found one.

Very little is known about the first labels because so few have survived to our present day. These appear to be the largest concentration, of a variety this old, ever found.

Labels like this one remind us that, when given the opportunity, people like a variety of food products no matter how far removed they are from the original source.

B & M obtained a registered trademark on July 31, 1877, under the Queen Brand. The trademark was a representation of the RISING SUN and used for canned lobsters.

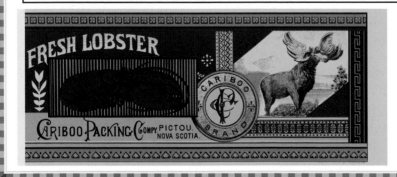

Lobster canning did not continue for long in the U. S. For those individuals who had eaten fresh lobster, canned lobster didn't quite measure up. The industry continued in Canada.

The label on the left was purchased and restored.

I'm not sure why a moose was used for **CARIBOO PACKING COMPY**. of **PICTOU, NOVA SCOTIA**.

This is one of two cans that displayed
PRIZE MEDALS.
These were **AWARDED** to **BURNHAM & MORRILL,**
by the **AMERICAN INSTITUTE** of **NEW YORK,**
and the **UNITED STATES CENTENNIAL,** of 1876.

Most of the labels found had registered a trademark. Others used a trademark without registering it. This label may have been before **B & M** had decided on what to use as a trademark.

45

DIRECTIONS.

Pudding– Take a quart of sweet milk, three eggs and a little salt, with flour enough to make a stiff batter, add a can of blueberries and steam the contents.

Cake-Take one cup of sour milk, one egg, little salt, two teaspoonfuls Cream Tarter, one of Soda, one cup Sugar, and flour to make a stiff batter. Stir in a half can of berries, pour into flat pans about two inches deep and bake in quick oven, split and butter.

Sauce– Warm thoroughly, adding sugar to taste.

Pie– Make paste as usual, using half can of blueberries, sweeten to taste.

BURNHAM & MORRILL

Proprietors of the Celebrated Brands of
MACHIAS BAY LOBSTERS,
PARIS SWEET CORN,
PARIS SUCCOTASH,
SCARBORO BEACH CLAMS.

Packers of all kinds of Meats, Fruits, Fish and Vegetables.

PORTLAND ME. U. S. A.

This is the only label to provide recipes for additional uses of their product.

This can rates a picture because it was the one reflecting the beam from my flash light.

The condition of this can gives more meaning to the term 'high and dry.'

There are no signs of rust on the outside, except for a tiny bit at the bottom.

The little piece of label remaining tells us it had a **TRADEMARK** and that it was from **BALTIMORE.**

These early cans were a heavier gauge metal, weighing between five and seven ounces. Modern cans of equivalent size weigh between three and four ounces.

This can is still shiny in the photograph.

Notice the soldering on the top of the can, which became the bottom when the label was applied. Soldering was done by hand at this time, therefore no two cans are identical.

One reason hand soldering continued for so many years was that the tin-smiths didn't give up without a fight. Canneries were broken into and the automated equipment was destroyed, and the canneries were burned.

47

ERIE PRESERVING CO.
Of **Buffalo, N.Y.**
Registered their Trademark
The word-symbol **ERIE**
#5,691 on March 5, 1878.

This would be their first design.
Notice the
HIGHEST CENTENNIAL AWARD
It also reads
TABLE GOODS
GUARANTEED
FINEST QUALITY

Many early canneries opened in upper New York State, not only because of the crops grown, but also because of the proximity to the Erie Canal. The Erie Canal opened on October 26, 1825, connecting Lake Erie with the Hudson River.

The food industry has always been at the mercy of the mode of transportation. At this period of history, growers had to be close enough to the canneries to get their produce there by horse and wagon before it lost its freshness. Canners in turn needed a sure supply of raw products before investing in a cannery in the first place. They also needed an economical means of transportation to get their finished product to market. If they were not by navigable water they could not open until the railroad laid a track to their particular area.

This can contained tomatoes. At first glance I thought this label was for peaches until a final cleaning revealed that the shape of the tomato along with the leaf and stem are consistent with some of the other tomato labels.

This one bean can is the only one found that had any indication that someone tried to heat the contents. The fact that the label didn't burn entirely, after catching on fire, attests to the durability of the paper.

These beans were one of the few food products that received its own patent. It is recorded in Volume 12, page 245, of the Official Gazette, U. S. Patent Office, Patent # 193,880 of Aug. 7, 1877. The patent was issued to W. K. Lewis for canning beans and pork. It is recorded as follows :

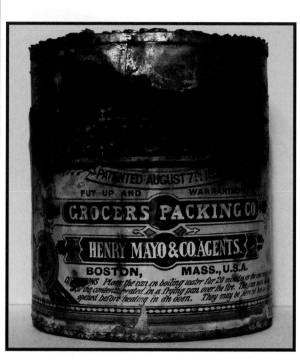

'The process, substantially as described, of putting up baked beans for the market, the same consisting in first parboiling the beans, then placing them in a can with pork, and hermetically sealing the can, and afterward subjecting the can containing the parboiled beans and the pork to the action of heated water or steam, whereby the same are prepared for immediate use.'

We found ten of these bean cans with the other 1882 cans, making it the second most eaten product.

If not for the wood chips and dry atmosphere, the bottom of this can is an example of the normal deterioration of tin cans. Even in dry conditions this is the outcome of not being on the chips. In spite of this it still survived, with its embossed lid, since 1882.

These cans, some in nearly new condition and others reduced to rust, were only a few feet apart.

Fortunately, pine wood has a natural oil that helps keep paper and metal eating bacteria controlled.

TRADE MARK
BOSTON
BAKED BEANS
PATENTED AUG. 7TH 1877
W.K. LEWIS
BOSTON.
This is the can that Kelly saw the date on that made us realize we had found something worth saving.

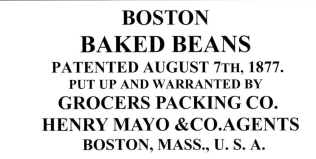

BOSTON
BAKED BEANS
PATENTED AUGUST 7TH, 1877.
PUT UP AND WARRANTED BY
GROCERS PACKING CO.
HENRY MAYO &CO.AGENTS
BOSTON, MASS., U. S. A.

DIRECTIONS   Place the can in boiling water for 20 minutes or the can may be opened and the contents heated in a frying pan over the fire. The can must always be opened before heating in an oven. They may be served hot or cold.

On either side of the bean pot we're given the following information:

UNDER THE PATENTED PROCESS ALONE CAN THE BEANS BE WARRANTED AS PERFECT AND TO KEEP IN ANY CLIMATE. BUYERS ARE HEREBY CAUTIONED, AS ALL INFRINGEMENTS ARE LIABLE TO SEIZURE.

CAUTION: NONE GENUINE WITHOUT "W. K. LEWIS, BOSTON BAKED BEANS, PATENTED AUGUST 7th 1877," STAMPED IN THE TOP OF EACH CAN WITH A LABEL BEARING THE BLUE RIBAND AND THE SEAL OF THE UNITED STATES.

*Riband is the old spelling of ribbon.

No 234. THE DINNER HOUR.

Courtesy of the COLORADO HISTORICAL SOCIETY

This would be a typical scene from the 1880's in the Colorado mountains. Rusting evidence in countless locations attests to the popularity of canned goods once they became available. If you could multiply this pile of cans by three, you would have an idea of the amount of cans we found under the 1882 house.

The second find of cans from 1892 or 1893, had nearly six times this amount even after they had been 'cleaned out.' The majority of them didn't fare much better than this pile probably did.

So far, this is the only photo we have seen which has a label that is identifiable from this time period. If not for already having the labeled cans to go by this would have just been a pile of unrecognizable cans.

If you came upon this site, and if no one else had been there, the embossed lids of these cans would likely be identifiable today, but paper labels needed a combination of special circumstances to survive.

It is highly unlikely that another cache of cans like the ones found from 1882 exists.

Notice the hand soldered caps on the ends of the cans.

Since finding the first labeled cans, any old photo that contained canned goods has been carefully studied with a magnifying glass with the hope of identifying a label. The bean pot on the **BOSTON BAKED BEANS** can (lower left corner) in this enlargement of the photo was easily identified. The second can to its right, with its open end facing forward, appears to be the other side of the same label. The smaller open can facing forward behind it may be a Borden's milk can. The other labels in this small sampling tell us there were many other beautiful and interesting labels of that time which may never be found.

This food is not what might first come into your mind. The following information from The U.S. Patent Office Book of March 26, 1878, gives us this information. Patent # 201,834 assigned to Wm W. Treat, of Watertown Mass., filed on November 23, 1876, reads:

Trademark #5,588 was registered on January 29, 1878, for MINCED FISH to William W. Treat of Watertown, Mass. The trademark is the **W. W. T. S.** found in the tail.

'Brief –Cured Fish and Potatoes are chopped into a hash, to which are added tallow and saltpeter. The compound is then placed in a can, hermetically sealed, and boiled accordingly to the well known Appert process, (Passed by the board of examiners-in-Chief.)'

'Claim-the process herein described of permanently preserving cured fish and potatoes together, as a commercial article of food for all climates, consisting in first washing the fish in tepid water and cleansing it of superfluous salt and other impurities, then reducing it to pulp, then mixing it with cooked hashed potatoes and raw chopped onions, tallow, condiments, and saltpeter, in substantially the proportions specified, and then, while warm, sealing the compound hermetically in cans and boiling, as described.'

Saltpeter was used as a preservative.

DIRECTIONS

TO FRY CAKES—Mix the contents of can well together, make into small pats, dredge with flour or meal if convenient, and fry brown in a pan or skillet over a brisk fire. Additional butter or lard may be used in frying if desired. Serve hot.

FOR FISHERMEN'S COBLER—Put the contents of a can into a pan or skillet, stir well together over a brisk fire, till hot and crispy; butter or lard may be used, as in the cakes.

FOR ALL TIMES—May be heated in the can before or after opening, by putting the can in boiling water twenty minutes, or over a slow fire.

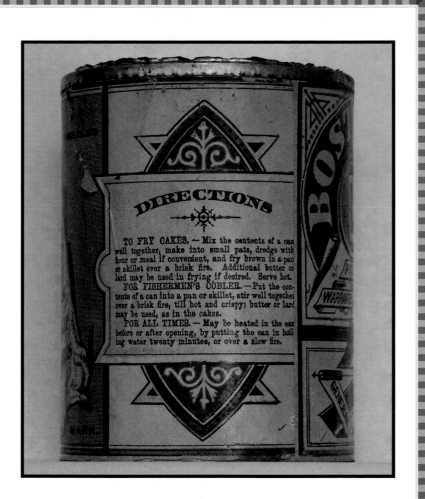

The Cod Fish Balls label is one of three different labels that recorded a date.
MARCH 26, 1878

The description as recorded in the patent book sounds like a fairly complete meal in a can, and apparently was quite favored by the inhabitants of Leadville. We were able to identify about a dozen cans from under the house as **CODFISH BALLS**, the most cans of any single product.

This can is indelibly written into Leadville history because of a mining claim. The claim was named **CODFISH BALLS**. I was told by long time resident and miner, Don Wilson, that it was named after what the owners were eating. This was further confirmed by information gleaned from Don L. Griswold's 'History of Leadville and Lake County,' 1996.

There was a court battle between the Louisville Mining Company and the Iron Mine Mining Company, over who had the rights to a body of ore that the Iron Silver Mining Co. had been extracting from their northernmost claim. This was the **CODFISH BALLS** claim.

The ore, though, was being removed underground from the Louisville's claim.

The court proceedings had become quite heated, when during the arguments an interesting suggestion was put forth by Judge Symes.

He proposed that the opposing sides could, "eat a diet of codfish balls to split the infernal thing in two." Evidently the eating of codfish balls caused repercussions. In the end the court sided with the Louisville Mining Company.

A map from 1901 of the Leadville mining area, giving the names of the mining claims including the **CODFISH BALLS** and **LOUISVILLE** claim, is on the next page. An enlarged inset that you are able to read is on the following page.

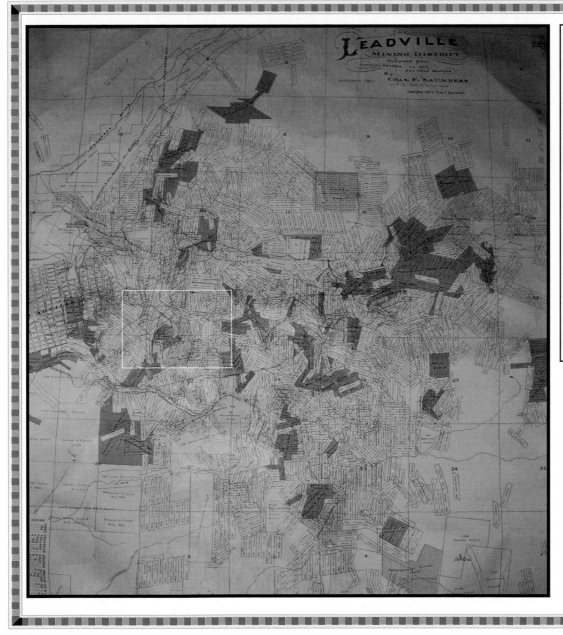

The original canvas map (not shown in its entirety), measures 32 x 44 inches. The insert on the next page takes up a 4 x 5 inch area of the map. Seeing the amount of claims in that one section helps you realize the amount of people that rushed to this area in such a short time. This created a need in food production to supply the demand. Later in the book more history of Leadville will appear. For now the fact that a food product from Boston, that hardly anyone today ever knew existed, was recorded on a map, attests to Leadville's history being tied into the preserving of early canning history.

This six and three quarter inch brass bell had been discarded in an old outhouse with a wide variety of other artifacts. It had probably been used as a signal bell for one of these many mines.

An envelope containing the coal delivery receipts from the John Harvey Coal Co. for the month of November 1894 was rescued from the snow during the winter of 1985. The building was being dismantled and the remaining contents were being discarded. The receipts took on added meaning with the story of the **CODFISH BALLS** and **LOUISVILLE** lawsuit, and the map. On the map, the **LOUISVILLE, CODFISH BALLS** and the **MAHALA** are found in the white boxes.

No. K 3577 OFFICE OF
JOHN HARVEY.
COAL DEALER.
Leadville, Colo., Nov 2 189 4
RECEIVED, One Load of COAL, Per Weigher's Receipt
For Louisville
4840 Pounds.
Smith & Gallaway

No. K 3580 OFFICE OF
JOHN HARVEY.
COAL DEALER.
Leadville, Colo., Nov 2 189 4
RECEIVED, One Load of COAL, Per Weigher's Receipt
For Mahala
4520 Pounds.
Geo Pritchard

These receipts from a few mines further confirm the continued activity in this area to help keep up the demand for the growing canning industry. Established cities were not the market for the earliest canned foods because if other food products were available the general population did not eat out of cans. Home canning was also practiced according to an 1870 newspaper article. The lack of fresh produce in this area at this period in time and the wealth mining created was why canneries from far and wide were shipping their canned goods to this area in great abundance.

No. K 3987 OFFICE OF
JOHN HARVEY.
COAL DEALER.
Leadville, Colo., Nov 19 189 4
RECEIVED, One Load of COAL, Per Weigher's Receipt
For Johnnie # 1
4620 Pounds.
John Murphy

One of Leadville's most well known individuals was the **'Unsinkable Molly Brown.'** The receipt above is one of eighteen found that recorded the delivery of 87,080 lbs. of coal between Nov. 17 and 28, of 1894, to the **Johnnie #1**. This was the mine that produced the wealth that enabled the **'Unsinkable Molly Brown'** to afford to be on the Titanic in 1912.

The claim is east of the map close-up.

Since the **'Little Johnny'** was a gold mine, they were still profitable and in operation after the silver crash of 1893.

The coal delivered was primarily used to fire the boilers that kept the pumps running to keep the water level down.

A worker was paid $4 a day to deliver 8 tons, which with loading and unloading was 16 tons. (Just like the song.)

This page of March 1893 from the 'time' book of the **Midnight Mine** gives several interesting facts from 1893. The miners made between $3.00 & $5.00 per day. For some reason one man named Frank Williams was paid $7.00 a day for eleven days. His name is recorded on the next page. Several did not have a day off the entire month. It required two pages to list the 71 miners that were employed in March 1893. By May the number had been reduced to 54. This book records nothing after this. They may have stopped temporarily because of the silver crash of 1893, but that wasn't until July. Perhaps they just changed time books. Whatever reason, there were many empty pages left.

The Midnight Mine was also a gold mine and in November of 1894 they were still ordering loads of coal. We found receipts for more than ten tons.

Many of the silver mines had continued in operation or had reopened.

The fourteenth name down on the ledger appears to be the same signature as the one shown on the coal delivery, shown below dated Nov. 2, 1894, from **JOHN HARVEY, COAL DEALER.**

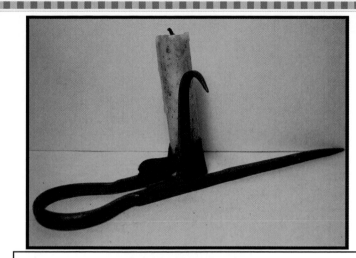

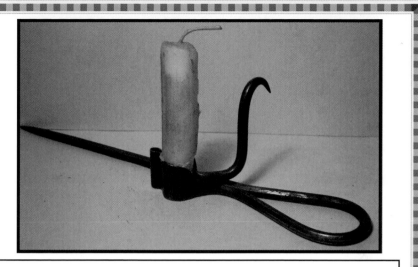

These miner's candle sticks were found in various locations in Leadville. The two above were found in our barn. The one below, with the stub of its original candle and covered with spilled paint, was found under a house during renovations.

The one on the lower right had been in a fire. They were hand made, therefore all are different. They could be hung from or driven into a timber, post, or a crack in the rock for light. The early candles would burn at different rates.

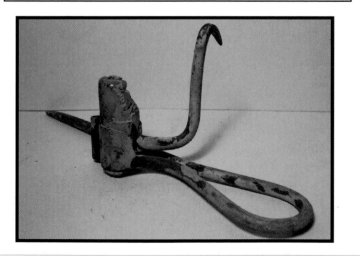

Hopefully some spares were carried so as not to get caught in the dark.

The dark candle was added later. Original candles appeared to be white.

Mining related activities and war opened the door for canned goods well before they were accepted by the general population. These labels would not have been found in other early mining areas because by the time they were designed most of the gold and silver rushes were over. In 1879 with the realization that the heavy ore that interfered with the extraction of gold was actually silver, the second rush was on to Leadville

.This commemorative token was made in remembrance of the men that toiled to remove the riches from the earth. The prospector is holding a rifle, and standing by his gear laden burro. The big year for the influx of miners and related job seekers was 1879. As the token says these individuals were called **A 79 ER.**
The side below reads:
A COLORADO PROSPECT
W. W. (?)CHISHOLM . LEADVILLE, COLORADO

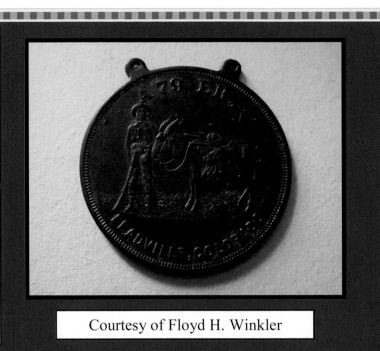

Courtesy of Floyd H. Winkler

The side on the left is loaded with detail. It is a cutaway view of a mine with a vertical shaft. Three men are seen on the surface, one with a wheelbarrow, and two operating the hoist to raise and lower the ore buckets, which also carried the men. Five miners are down in the mine doing various tasks. At the bottom, one man is holding a drill steel as the other is preparing to hit it with a double jack. Two have picks, and the other appears to be placing a device for lighting. Two other lighting devices are seen on each side of the shaft above the miners. The spikes protruding from the miners heads are the artists depiction of light. The light from 1879 would come from candles.

A BIRD'S EYE VIEW of
LEADVILLE, COLO. in 1882.

This was Leadville in the year the first cans were
discarded by the workers that built the house.

LEADVILLE, COLO.
1882.

RICHARDSON & ROBBINS
CHICKEN
DOVER, DEL. U.S.A.

The printer of this label was the
RUSSELL MORGAN CO. CIN. O.
They began printing in 1867.

A.B. Robbins began canning processed
food in Dover in 1856.

This may have been one of the companies
involved in lawsuits with Libby, McNeill & Libby
over the tapered can.

They Registered their Trademark
#7,702 on September 23, 1879:
'The letters and character R&R and the
Arrow connecting them together.'

Some of the information on the label reads:
For Travelers   For   Excursionists

Contents of this can of superior quality——

**It is desirable, when possible, to place the
Can on Ice before using.**

For (unknown)   **For   Sportsmen**

Cut close to the edge either side or bottom, and then contents will slide out whole. Notice the hand with the pointing finger. I don't know how early this symbol was used to point, indicating directions, but it is one symbol that has remained the same through the years.

Richardson & Robbins, an Underwood brand, pioneered the hermetically sealed can.

Whoever opened this can started on the wrong end with something besides a can opener, realized the chicken wouldn't slide out and then opened it on the other end.

The top of this can is embossed:
RICHARDSON & ROBBINS
DOVER, DEL. U. S. A.

The yellow box above clearly states:
NO SOLDER
USED ON THE INSIDE
OF THIS CAN

By the time this Label was printed they knew that lead was harmful, and on this can it appears they did a pretty good job of keeping the solder on the outside.

This box below is on the other side.

KEOKUK, IOWA, was a cannery center in the Midwest.

It is the southern most town in Iowa, situated on the Mississippi river, making it an ideal location for shipping in the early 1880's.

This label contributed its back half to the nest of the mouse. The small part of the corner that remains shows the beauty of the design.

An identifying label number (1434) is in the lower left corner. It's not seen in the photo.

Researching a subject that very little has been written about does at times seem a little futile. About the time you decide you have found all you can, surprisingly something else shows up in an unexpected place. During my research about the Iowa canneries, I remembered an old newspaper found taped to the bottom of a drawer of a gentleman's hat box dresser, from Fairfield, Iowa.

The dresser had belonged to a great aunt who came to Colorado from Iowa in the early 1890's. I don't know when it came into my mother's possession, but I remember it from the 50's. The newspaper wasn't discovered until 1998 when I inherited the dresser. It wasn't until the end of 2004 we carefully looked through the paper hoping to find any reference to canned goods. This small article on Canning Tomatoes was found. The paper was **The Fairfield Ledger,** of September 15, 1870. Fairfield is about 50 air miles N. W. of the location of the tomato cannery in Keokuk, Iowa.

The directions for canning, using the hole-in-the-cap cans, just happened to be found in the oldest newspaper we have. The coincidence of this article being in one of the few old papers already in our possession was incredible.

The pointing finger for directions was also in use in 1870. Here it's saying 'look here.'

Canning Tomatoes.—For the benefit of those who like "sugar in their'n," we publish the following recipe for canning tomatoes:

"Scald and skin the tomatoes; drain off all the juice; fill the can till it weighs two pounds; add one large tablespoonful of syrup, made in the following manner: To one gallon of water, one pound and a half of salt, and the same of sugar; seal the cans and set them in boiling water thirty minutes; open the vent for the escape of the gas and seal again."

☞ There is no risk in buying of G. A. UNKRICH. He warrants his Coffee, Tea, Sugar, Fish, &c., and all at the lowest market price.

This red, white, blue and black label was one of two different cans found that were printed by the **HINDS KETCHAM & CO.** of New York. It has been thought by some that the Hinds Ketcham & Co. printed the first colored labels about 1880. With the new information speaking from this cache of cans it's established that the Forbes Co. of Boston was printing them in 1876, the Crump 5 Color Label Press of New York, by 1877, and at least a few others by 1879.

Trademark #3,100, registered for Fruit Butter on Nov. 26, 1875, by J. O. Schimmel and Co. of Philadelphia, Pa. gives an even earlier date for color. The trademark reads: "A representation of fruits consisting of peaches, apples, pears, cherries, quinces, strawberries, interspersed with rose-buds or other flowers and leaves in natural Colors ."

A variation of this trademark was often used.

Where this can came from is missing from the label, but it was probably from Lansing, New York, just north of Ithaca. It is the **IMPERIAL BRAND** and it contained **TOMATOES**. This can looks as if it had been thrown away and its label chewed off a few days ago, not over 122 years ago.

Some of the history of printing, regarding labels around this time period was trademark # 663 for Calico Prints, registered by Coffin & Altemus of Philadelphia, on Feb. 20, 1872.

Trademark #637 on Jan. 23, 1872, for Labels and Show-Cards was registered by Samuel Crump of New York.

A patent was issued to George C. Lewis on April 25, 1876, for the preparation of photographs for reception of colors. Patent # 176,653.

The patent reads:

'The process herein described of preparing the surfaces of photographic pictures for the reception of coloring material by applying to the same a coating of gummy or gelatinous substance combined with honey or other hygroscopic material, substantially as set forth.'

A few years ago I read about this process in an old book. (I have yet to re-find the book.) After the book reported that an Irishman named Lewis patented this process, it next said: "What this will do for the food labeling industry is yet to be seen."

It may well be that the later ones of these labels are the results of his process.

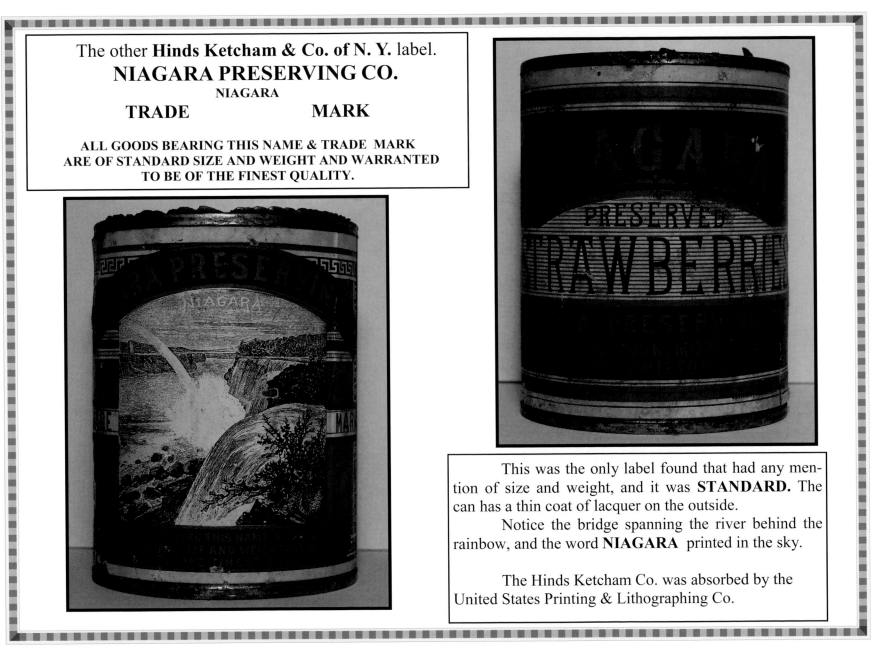

The other **Hinds Ketcham & Co. of N. Y.** label.

NIAGARA PRESERVING CO.

NIAGARA

TRADE   **MARK**

ALL GOODS BEARING THIS NAME & TRADE MARK
ARE OF STANDARD SIZE AND WEIGHT AND WARRANTED
TO BE OF THE FINEST QUALITY.

This was the only label found that had any mention of size and weight, and it was **STANDARD.** The can has a thin coat of lacquer on the outside.

Notice the bridge spanning the river behind the rainbow, and the word **NIAGARA** printed in the sky.

The Hinds Ketcham Co. was absorbed by the United States Printing & Lithographing Co.

Lockport is about twenty miles east of Niagara falls on the Erie canal. They were one of the first companies to use metal containers. The Niagara Preserving Co. went bankrupt in 1909.

The rock building used by the **Niagara Preserving Co.** back in the 1840's is now the Lockport Locks and Erie Canal Cruises Inc.

The above lid was with the can labels, but I was unable to find its other half. I can't say for sure what it was, but I would guess it was boot polish.

On January 28, 1879, **BOYER & CO**. of **33 N. FRONT ST., PHILA, PA**. registered their label, #1,845 for **IMPROVED FRENCH BLACKING.**

It is a paper label pasted on the metal lid.

The spelling of **JANY** caught my attention.

This was one of the few products that were found that had registered a label instead of a trademark.

These two bean cans are the only ones from the same company, which contained different products.

According to the picture, the **REFUGEE BEANS** are a thicker bean than the **FINE STRINGLESS BEANS.**

The bottom yellow boxes are also different. The one below includes **PACKED AT** and **MONROE CO**.

CURTICE BROTHERS of **ROCHESTER, N. Y.** applied for their trademark on Nov. 6, 1876, and received it Nov. 21, 1876. This represents one of the shortest spans of time for the process of receiving a trademark. Their trademark was 'an **OCTAGONAL** figure.'

This label survived in fabulous condition. The preservation is good enough that you are able to read the printing right off the label.

The details and colors of this label have defied all rules of natural deterioration. It's a good thing that most cans and labels return to rust and dust like they were supposed to, otherwise we would be buried in tin cans. It's also nice that a few didn't.

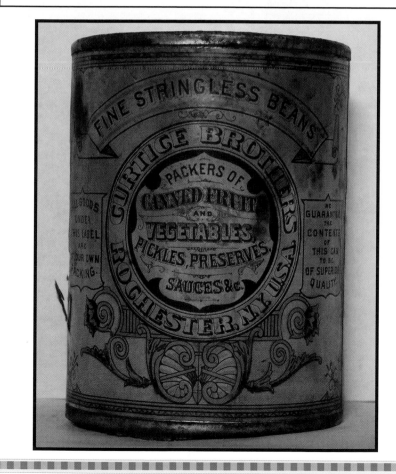

It is necessary to study many of these labels to appreciate the beauty in the art. Notice that the four corners in the panels of this label are two different designs. The lettering has a number of different styles. Extra details are everywhere.

73

This one can gets to be larger
than it really is because it is so special.

This is the oldest dated label on any of the cans. Reading from the bottom up, in the yellow border, in light blue letters, it reads :

LABEL REGISTERED 1876.

We found three of these Refugee Bean cans with readable dates. It was more than a year after finding them, as I was going over them with a magnifying glass, that the date was discovered.

From this view you can clearly see their trademark, the **octagonal** figure. It is used three times on each label.

The small blue lettering is the printer.
Forbes Co. Boston

The Stringless Beans label on page 72, had neither the date nor the printer recorded.

Older labeled cans do exist. Pictures of three, dating from 1874, are found in THE TIN CAN BOOK by HYLA M. CLARK, published in 1977. Many of the pictures in the book are in color, but the three from 1874 are shown in black and white.

THE LITTLE OLD TIN CAN

Dedicated to Commodore Daniel M. Heeken
of Cincinnati.

Regard the little old tin can,
That held some sort of food,
It may have been just beans or soup,
Or prunes that had been stewed,
Or caviar or mushrooms,
To delight the inner man,
And then the raging floods engulfed
    That little old tin can.

Placid streams turned into torrents,
Swelled by rains o'er Man's control,
Hurled ahead their mighty tonnage,
Tearing at the very soul,
Of helpless city, town, and hamlet,
Dealing death to beast and man,
Not a thing escaped destruction,
    Save that little old tin can.

When the rivers calmed to normal,
And the wreckage cleared away,
Out of all the filthy debris,
Just one thing allowed to stay,
Quite unnamed and maybe dented,
Yet food wholly fit for man,
Safely sterilized and healthful,
    In that little old tin can.

Just a scrub with soap and water,
Takes away the silt and mold,
A container and a label,
And it's ready to be sold;
The floods of nineteen thirty-seven,
Threw terror into man,
Yet couldn't harm the contents
    Of that little old tin can.

WINTHROP C. ADAMS

Cambridge, Mass.

HANTHORN & CO of **ASTORIA, OREGON.**
registered their trademark on Dec. 11, 1877. The Trademark is the picture below.

'The figure of a hand, with a portion of the arm halfway up to the elbow. In the hand is clasped a fish.'

This can was liberally coated with lacquer. The purpose was to prevent the can from showing rust prematurely. It was successful beyond their wildest dreams.

To continue preserving the labels they must be kept out of the sunlight and away from moisture.

This is one of the only labels that did not go completely around the can. After finding these cans we have come across other salmon cans, and found that this label would fit perfectly on these smaller cans. This can used by the Hanthorn Company is larger than any other salmon cans that we have seen. The Hanthorn Company was likely among the seven early Columbia River canneries that became Bumble Bee in 1899.

The information printed between the panels reads:
CRUMP 5 COLOR LABEL PRESS N. Y.
H. S. CROCKER & CO. AG-S. S. F.
(Agents)

Here we see two more of the eye catching labels printed by **THE COLONIST** of Victoria, B. C.

As salmon runs began to diminish along the Columbia River the industry began to look north. 1875 saw the first salmon cannery along the Fraser River, British Columbia. Two years later the first salmon cannery in Puget Sound began operations in Mukilteo, Washington.

Courtesy of The ROYAL B. C. MUSEUM

Courtesy of The ROYAL B. C. MUSEUM

This CARIBOO BRAND for FRASER RIVER SALMON did use a caribou in its design.

The wording above the **SALMON** is: CAUGHT AT THE MOUTH OF THE RIVER & PACKED FRESH FROM THE SALT WATER.

Cariboo was the Canadian spelling of caribou.

| Fisherman Sitting On the Dock   By R. L. (Jack) Clark |

This scene could fit any of the coastal cities and towns that would have had a fishing fleet and a salmon cannery. The wooden sailing vessels were used on both coasts to not only fish, but also to transport cargo that would include early canned goods.

The barrels stacked on the dock were how countless products were shipped in bulk to not only the coastal towns, but also the cities, towns and mining camps of the West.

In January of 2005, I returned to Leadville, and was able to gather some additional material to tie the labels and lore to Leadville. I have been pleasantly surprised as to how many people have wonderful memories to relate when cans and labels are inserted into a conversation.

If I could make it to the Golden Burro Restaurant by 6:30 for breakfast, I would share a table with Morris (mentioned earlier). He would listen to what I had written and tell me related history. He remembered that during the depression years, many of the food products, from candy to oysters, came to the stores in barrels. He and his friends would take the discarded barrels apart and tie the individual boards to their feet for skis. From Morris I learned that the demand for canned milk diminished during his youth with over a dozen dairies starting up in this one small area. Today the dairies are gone. This pattern was typical of most areas of the nation. Canneries have had a similar history.

Another use of labels that is still in effect today is their use as premiums. For many years the paper milk bottle tops could get you into the theater. During the depression years, Morris and his friends used the food can labels of F. F. O. G. (Fight For Old Glory) to get into the theater. They usually only had enough for one ticket, so one boy would go in, then unlock the side door and let all of the other kids in. Instead of being tossed out they just had to go down to the front and sit on orange crates.

SALMON
PACKED BY
N. PARDINI & CO.
SAN FRANCISCO, CAL.

Overland Brand probably picked their name from the Overland Mail Company, which was formed in 1862. Most people today recognize the name as the stage line from old Western movies. They controlled the entire overland stage business from Kansas to California until 1866, when they were displaced by Wells, Fargo & Co.

OVERLAND BRAND was known for cigars, but they had their first design, 'A gray 1870's steam engine,' on this salmon can.

This is another example of a can coated with lacquer. It does attest to the lasting quality of the lacquer on the metal it protected.

In the corners of the label are the words:

CALIFORNIA   **SPRING**

This can was not found with the others, but was discovered in Des Moines, Iowa, when walls were uncovered in an old hotel.

It showed up on eBay in December of 2001. By this time we were curious as to how high the bidding would go, so we joined in. Our last bid was made in the final seconds, and we paid $102.50 for an empty tin can.

I haven't confirmed just how old this label is, but it has all of the characteristics of the Pre-1882 cans.

Later on eBay another salmon can from Alaska sold for $405.00, and an oyster can from Baltimore for $208.00. They had no accompanying history.

Many of the lithographed tin containers were meant to be saved. Not so, the food containing tin can.

Even though they were meant to be discarded after emptying, the illustrators used wonderful graphics, reminiscent of the early trade signs, to get noticed. Nevertheless, discarded they were, and their life expectancy was short. Rare is the time you find even one.

The printer was the
BANCROFT CO. S . F.
They were in business
by 1877.

COLTON
FRUIT PRESERVING CO.
COLTON, CAL.
C. ADOLPHE LOW & CO.
GENERAL AGENTS.
SAN FRANCISCO.
SELECTED RASPBERRY JELLY
EXTRA QUALITY
FRUITS OF CALIFORNIA

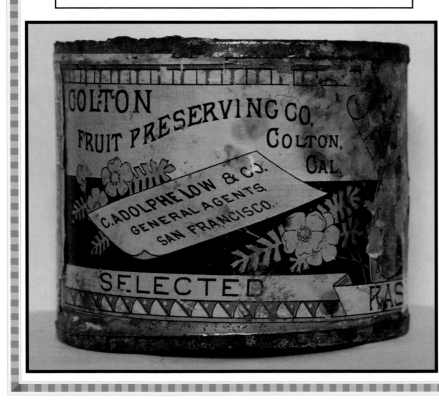

This is a wonderful example of early advertising telling a story.

You have the picture of the cannery and a steam locomotive for delivery, although shown with a passenger car. An orchard is in the background, with the little girl carrying fruit in her apron, accompanied by her dog.

Watch for the girl and her dog on a later can.

The designers of this Label went all out to get your attention. The designs are different all the way around the can. The label has fruits, flowers, a bird, extra graphics, a train, and the appeal of the little girl with her dog. This is the type of advertising that would appeal to a wide variety of customers.

This design of fruit is a variation of the trademark recorded on page 68.

The tiny print under
RASPBERRY JELLY is the printer,
SCHMIDT LABEL & LITH. CO. S.F

Colton is south of San Bernardino, California.

This Historic Business Card was found tossed away with the cans. Research in the City Directories at the Leadville Public Library establish that the information on the business card was, word for word, the same as that recorded for the year 1882.

CARSON
STAGE & EXPRESS LINE
SERVING TWIN LAKES, EVERETTS, INDEPENDENCE, ASPEN AND ASHCROFT.
OFFICE, 214 WEST CHESTNUT ST.
LEADVILLE, COLORADO

CHAS. LANG.   J. C. CARSON.   J. E. SLAGLE.
Agent, Leadville   Proprietor   Agent, Aspen

The background of this card has a stagecoach with two horses, and a driver with a whip.

LEADVILLE HISTORY

In 1880 John C. Carson was working as an express man, and by 1881, in partnership with a man named Wales, formed the Leadville, Twin Lakes and Independence Stage Line at 214 W. Chestnut St.

214 W. Chestnut was also the address for the Charles Lang Saloon, and as the business card tells us, he was the Leadville agent.

By 1882 without Wales, Carson was hauling supplies over 12,093 ft. Independence Pass to Aspen and the silver mining area of Ashcroft.

Everetts was the stage stop on the eastern side, and Independence was the stage stop on the western side of Independence Pass .

If you have driven the paved highway over Independence Pass between Aspen and Leadville, you can imagine the stamina of the men involved in starting up and operating this stage line. Even today this pass is only open between Memorial Day and the first major snowfall in autumn. These men had as examples others who had accomplished equal or greater things before them. Years before this supplies were hauled into the mountains from Denver through South Park by wagon over 13,110 ft. Mosquito Pass. (Don't try this route with a passenger car.)

By 1884 Carson had moved from the Saloon to 108 West 4th St., four blocks north. In 1887 he expanded his stage line to include Glenwood Springs. According to the 1888 City Directory he was no longer in business.

Another interesting piece of history regarding the 'Carson Stage Line' occurred on Christmas Eve of 1886. The 'Carson Stage Line' and the 'Denver and Rio Grande Express Company' were instrumental in sponsoring a fight in Leadville between the "Great John L." Sullivan and the former U.S. title holder, Steve Taylor. The fight was over in the third round by Taylor backing into the corner signaling Sullivan to stop. Sullivan was given a diamond charm by the sponsors.

Another name that was found with the cans was **Clinton Reed** the subscriber of the July 8, 1882, Chicago Legal News.

In 1882 Clinton Reed had a law practice with J.B. Belford at 107 West 3rd, in Leadville.

Someone, working on the house where the cans were found, probably picked up the paper from his office or trash, and after they were finished with it, threw it under the house with their empty tin cans.

While researching about Clinton Reed there was one bit of history that attracted my attention and it made me think of the 'Unsinkable Molly Brown.' Molly Brown was always trying to be accepted by 'High Society,' but until she survived the 'Titanic' in 1912 it had always eluded her. After that 'Denver society' finally did accept her.

The history I came across was from 1888. Leadville, which was as far removed from High Society as you could get geographically, still put forth great efforts to have the same functions. A certain 'High Tea' was a Rose Tea given by Mrs. George Goldthwaite, and among others, it was attended by J.B. Henslee and Clinton Reed.

J.B. Henslee was at first an ore buyer and by 1888 was in real estate. One thing of interest for us about J.B. Henslee, is that he lived in the house my family and I owned and restored.

****

What are the odds of this small piece of newspaper having both the date and the subscribers name preserved?

This coal receipt signed by Mr. Henslee was found behind the floor trim of our home during restoration work.

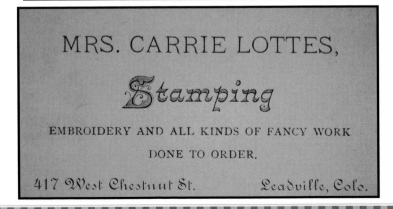

Another point of interest is that Mrs. Goldthwaite was the wife of Judge George Goldthwaite who presided over the trial of the people vs. Doc Holiday in August of 1884. The trial was the result of Doc Holiday's last gunfight, resulting in the wounding of a man during a card game. He was acquitted of attempted murder. Holiday came to Leadville sometime after the October 26, 1881, "Gunfight at the OK Corral" in Tombstone, Arizona.

He left Leadville shortly after the trial and moved to Glenwood Springs.

Leadville newspapers also printed labels, advertising fliers and business cards. These two business cards from the 1870's or 1880's are outstanding examples of their work. These two businesses were across the street from each other.

The card above shows the diversity of the services offered at one business. The advertising for groceries is of special interest here.

Newspapers can help us establish a date on found objects. These small pieces of newspaper are three of several pieces found with the cans. Below in the right column, at the bottom is:

**Denver, Colo.,
July 1st, 1882.**

Sometimes you find an entire page with no dates at all. Other times a tiny piece like the one on the right contain several dates. This was the local paper of **July 12, 1882.**

The dirt covered piece on the bottom right is what most of the pieces looked like. 122 year old newsprint does not clean well.

THE LEADVILLE REVEILLE- -SUPPLEMENT
LEADVILLE, COLORADO, AUGUST 31,1878

A large part of Leadville was constructed within a two year period and 1878 was the first of the two. This is the only known example of Leadville's first newspaper. Richard S. Allen printed the first paper on Feb. 23, 1878. The price was ten cents a copy. The last issue of The Leadville Reveille was Jan. 8, 1880.

This was one of the newspapers used for insulation on a wall of an 1878 miner's cabin located in our backyard.

Here is another piece of newspaper that was found with the cans. It is shown to further confirm the date of the oldest labels. This is a larger piece of the one that had the subscriber's name (Clinton Reed) stuck on it. The name of the paper, the **CHICAGO LEGAL NEWS**, was a pretty good indication that Mr. Reed was an attorney.

Immediately above **Contents** the location and date are printed:
CHICAGO, JULY 8, 1882.

Colorado Daily Chieftain
PUEBLO, COLORADO, THURSDAY , AUGUST 29, 1878.

This newspaper was also on an interior wall and recovered during restoration of the two room miner's cabin. Nothing was found under the cabin because of its age. All supplies at this time were transported by teams and wagons which didn't leave much to be thrown away. We did find things in the yard and under other structures.

A small notice in this paper said there were plans for a direct route, by wagon, from this city (Pueblo) to Leadville. (This route was likely Weston Pass.)

It was also interesting that an article about the expansion of The Denver & Rio Grande railroad, which would reach Leadville in 1880, is on the front page. The last stretch of this route to Salt Lake City through Glenwood Canyon wasn't completed until 1887.

Another entry in the paper was a full page of over 65 cattle brands of Southeastern Colorado ranches. The 2X4 brand was of interest, since most of the things were found during construction, therefore I have included it here.

These six parts of pages are all that remained of the brochure found with the cans. We didn't immediately grasp what it was, but couldn't imagine anyone advertising their maids. After a search through the City Directories for the years 1879 thru 1883, and finding no listing for **JACKMAN'S Lodging House,** and knowing that the only businesses not listed were the brothels, we now knew what was being advertised. It was a little surprising that they were advertised, but there were dozens of brothels and over a hundred saloons vying for patronage, in this mountain town.

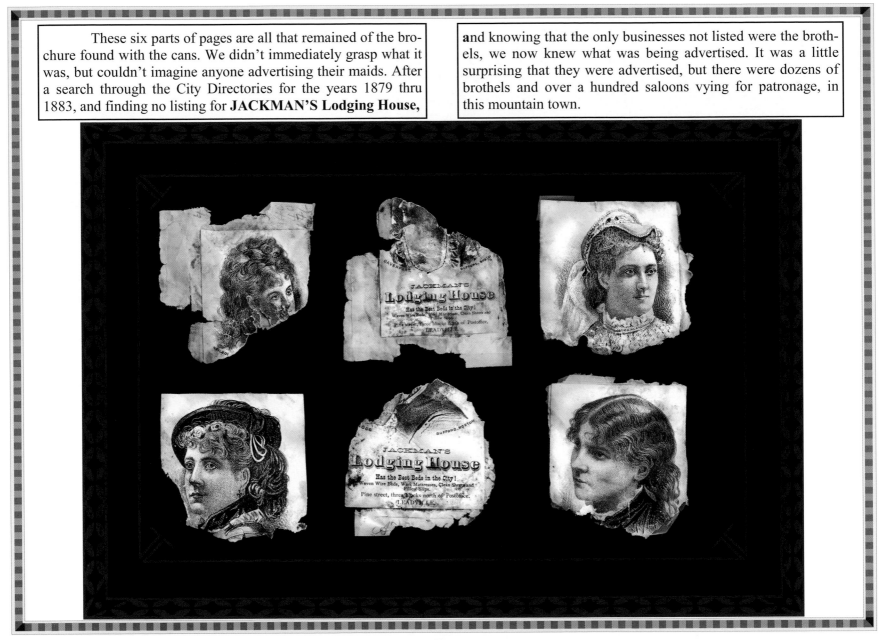

These two pictures are the front and back of the same page of the brochure. What was done was to paste individual business cards on each side of the page, and bind the pages together. They were bound at the top, so that they opened vertically instead of horizontally. That is why the top of one card and the bottom of the other card is missing due to disintegration.

The two words, **BUFFORD, BOSTON,** must be the printer, and the names that we are able to see, **DAVENPORT**, and probably **NEILSON**, and **KELLOGG** could be the names the girls went by. (Not very exotic.)

The card is printed as recorded below.

JACKMAN'S
Lodging House
Has the Best Beds in the City!
Woven Wire Beds, Wool Mattresses, Clean Sheets
and
Pillow Slips.
Pine street, three blocks north of Postoffice.
LEADVILLE.

This newspaper from October 4, 1879, was found under another house after the first cans with the labels, along with the brochure of the brothel, were found. The story in the center column seemed to fit the picture of this young woman from the brochure.

This article probably reveals the lives of many of the girls of the brothels quite accurately. It definitely removes any supposed glamour the movies sometimes depict.

The article is printed on the next page.

THE DAILY CHRONICLE

Leadville, Colorado, Saturday Evening, October 4, 1879

ROSE WHITE

****

The Woman Who Caused The Death of Slygh

"Oh God! Little I Thought That I Should Come To This."

The body of Robert B. Slygh, who shot himself through the heart, as fully narrated in last evening's CHRONICLE, is lying at Roger's morgue this afternoon along side of the body of the suicide Gordon. They are both fine looking young men, and both killed themselves because they both loved a woman. The body of Slygh will be sent to his friends in Grand Rapids, Michigan, tomorrow morning. Rose White, the girl that Slygh loved beyond endurance, was found in her room on State street, adjoining the one in which her lover took his life. As to the story that she has attempted to commit suicide last evening, she said that her head had troubled her by spells for two or three years and that the occurrence of yesterday had given her an acute attack of the difficulty. While thus affected she had wandered unconsciously to the Leadville Cemetery where found.

She had no idea of taking her own life. There the abandoned woman in a low sad tone of voice and with her eyes cast upon the floor as if her thoughts were far away from this dismal camp, began to tell the story of her eventful life. "I know I am very wicked; I know that I am the cause of Roberts death; I feel very sad on account of his poor mother from the letters she wrote to Robert; He used to let me read them all; They were filled with advice and counsel such as none but a good Christian mother could give; And how sad will be the life of that good woman now, and I am the cause of her sorrow; I know I am; once I was better than I am now; I wish I was better still; but I am lost; my father told me never to darken his door. He was offended because I married Johnson. Johnson was a streetcar conductor, and father said his habits were not good, but I loved him, and I thought I could win him from his wicked ways. That was only a few years ago. See what I am now. O, God! Little I thought that I should come to this. Yes I had a good education; I was reared in a Christian home; I know what is meant by good society, I know my degradation; I despise myself. Yet why am I here? I despise the depraved men who I am compelled to caress. See my condition now. In an hour I must play the gay and frivolous coquet or starve. None of my people know where I am. Mother thinks me dead. Better were it had I died ere I ever came to this. Oh, yes, the girls are all kind to me. Fallen women are better friends to each other than is ever known among the virtuous and respected. Perhaps father would take me home if he knew all. But I could not bare to face my people."

Leadville's notorious State Street before 1880. The girl in the 1879 newspaper article worked on this street. The girls from the brochure worked two blocks north. Other businesses also thrived in the same area. A theater is on the left and the mule team is in front of the New York Hotel, probably unloading produce for the grocery store next door.

Canned goods were not listed in a local advertisement for groceries in early 1879, but were mentioned in The Leadville Chronicle of October 4, 1879.

The timing of the rush of '79' provided the perfect setting for a fledgling canning industry with its newly designed colored labels. Here was an instant market with a need for a huge supply of food that could not be obtained locally. All that was needed was a way to get it there economically.

COLORADO MOUNTAIN HISTORY COLLECTION   Lake County Public Library, Leadville, Colorado

Chestnut Street in 1879, looking west.
A grocery store is located to the west of the book store on the corner.

Leadville's Chestnut Street in 1879, looking east towards the mining district. Chestnut began as the main street, but would soon be surpassed by Harrison Avenue.

All materials for construction were either milled locally from native forests or hauled in by wagons or pack animals. The railroad had not yet arrived.

Harrison Avenue looking south in 1879. The first telephone exchange in the U. S. had opened in 1878 in New Haven, Conn., and Leadville was not far behind. There were four cross arms on the poles before 1880.

The Tabor Opera House is under construction on the left. It was completed in less than one hundred days. This sixty foot brick structure is the only one, of four opera houses that Tabor had built, that is still standing.

COLORADO MOUNTAIN HISTORY COLLECTION   Lake County Public Library, Leadville, Colorado

This is Leadville's Harrison Avenue in the early 1880's, looking north. The Opera House had been completed in 1880 and was already advertising cigars and beer. The sign is still readable 125 years later. The number of cross arms on the telephone poles had increased to eighteen.

Goods from near and far, including canned foods, were now arriving by rail. The Denver & Rio Grande Railroad completed the line to Leadville in June of 1880. It was a big enough event that Ulysses S. Grant arrived on the first train. Seven more years would pass before the line was completed to Aspen. The silver that had been stockpiled, because of the high cost of shipping, could now be shipped out by rail. The arrival of the railroad to Aspen in November of 1887, also explained why the Carson Stage Line (on p. 86) ceased to exist by 1888.

The same means of transportation that made shipping silver from the mining towns economically feasible also made the importing of canned goods into the towns affordable.

In the years before the railroads arrived a can of beans could sell for one dollar a can. Afterwards in some areas the price dropped to less than fifteen cents a can. This would explain why construction workers could afford to be eating such a variety of canned food at Leadville in 1882.

This is a view, looking northwest, of East 4th Street from an undated photo. Most of these homes were built in 1878 and 1879. A few can still be identified today, but most have been replaced or changed enough to no longer be recognizable. The average house was built on a twenty-five foot lot, and in many cases the houses were twenty-four feet wide. The exterior walls had to be completely finished before being put in place. Like many quickly built towns, Leadville had it's share of fires, but the town still survived mostly intact.

The house in the white box became our home in 1984. Many of the treasures identified in these pages came from this address. It was under a house similar to these that the cans were found. Only in an area of low humidity would there be any chance of metal and paper surviving together under a structure.

The wooden sidewalks yielded thousands of coins and other small treasures when they were replaced.

COLORADO MOUNTAIN HISTORY COLLECTION   Lake County Public Library, Leadville, Colorado

This early photo shows an important means of transporting goods in the years before the railroads reached the cities of the West. The pack animals were able to carry a huge amount of goods without injury.

It was not uncommon for a burro to live to fifty years of age in relatively good health. They were well cared for by most of their owners and provided an invaluable service for the miners in the pursuit of their livelihood.

Before 1880 teams and wagons like these were the main way to transport supplies. For decades afterwards they were used to move the freight around the mining areas.

In the late 1960's a story was related to us by an early resident of Lake County, Colorado.

Sometime after 1900 Piers Paddock, born about 1885, was hauling logs into Leadville in a wagon similar to the one above. He came upon Baby Doe Tabor walking along the road. She waved him down and demanded that he give her a ride into town. Instead of climbing up in the front, which could have given the impression that they were together, she chose to sit on the logs at the back of the wagon. All went well until the wagon hit a mud hole in the road, thereby ejecting Mrs. Tabor off the logs and into the mud. Piers said: "You never heard such swearing from a woman in your life." I asked: "What did you do then?" He answered: "I was afraid to even look back, and I pretended I didn't hear her. I did my best to take a different route into town from then on." Only her pride was hurt.

THE SECOND CAN FIND

Thinking back on past events you realize how timing plays such an important part in the outcome of everything. If I had come across the first batch of cans earlier in time, they probably would have been in the same condition, but would I have even saved them?

The second batch of cans had been seen by an individual looking for old bottles under a structure in the 1970's, but old cans with labels were not what he was looking for. I was told that he just shoved them out of the way in his search for bottles and other items.

It was comparable to the early prospectors of the Leadville area that were looking for gold. The silver they encountered was just a heavy metal that got in the way.

Some years later the bottle digger started thinking about what he had seen earlier, and in the early 1990's he returned to the site, only to be told by the home owner that the cans had been cleaned out in another effort to search for bottles. I was told they were gone.

I started thinking that cleaned out could have a different meaning for various individuals. I then contacted the new owner to see if I could get permission to look under this structure to make sure for myself that I was not missing some deteriorating piece of history. Permission was granted.

Access to the underside of the building had to be from the inside through a hole in the floor. The opening in the floor was so small I had to completely exhale to get my chest through it, a quick reminder as to what was required to get to the earlier cans. To my surprise, cleaned out meant what I had hoped for. The majority were gone, but not all. The bottom layer of cans was still there, although in pretty bad shape. Some though did have enough of their labels remaining to fill another segment in the early history of canneries and their products.

Among the pre-1882 labels the closest cannery to Leadville was Grand Island, Nebraska. This pile of cans, for the most part, came from closer canneries, that did not exist in 1882. Only three labels had a connection with the first labeled cans found.

Another more extensive search under the same building in January of 2005 resulted in revising several pages in the history of these labels.

The following pages contain what was left of the labels, and the history that goes with them.

The **Maryland Brand** registered their first trademark on November 30, 1875. "The representation of the coat-of-arms of the State of Maryland, surrounded by a border supported at its dexter and sinister sides by oysters exposed in the open shell, the said border being surmounted by the representation of an eagle. The motto conceals the bottom of the border as shown. Over the whole are arranged, in an arch, the words **'Maryland Brand.'"**

This label has changed some since 1875, it no longer has an eagle or oysters, but it still has the coat-of-arms and **'Maryland Brand,'** in a different location.
packed by
**THOS. J. MYER & CO. at
BALTIMORE, MD.
STRING BEANS**
Thomas J. Myer & Co. began processing peaches with syrup in hermetically sealed tin cans in the 1850's.

These cans and labels are not shown for their lasting beauty, but for their history. The Cutting Packing Co. began using the representation of a **Griffin** in 1858, but did not register the trademarks, #18,119 and 18,120, for dried and canned goods, until July 1, 1890.

Although in much worse condition, these cans have a story of their own that continues the early history of the food canning industry.

Even with the rust destroying the can and label many of the details can still be deciphered. The **Griffin** is seen with the signature of the *Cutting Packing Co.* in the rectangular box above it. **ESTABLISHED 1858** is in the circle on the right. The tiny writing to the left of the beak contains the same words as those in the picture on the left. **NO GOODS GENUINE UNLESS BEARING THIS TRADEMARK & SIGNATURE. ESTABLISHED 1858.**

Cutting Packing Co.

Just under the **Griffin** is **TRADEMARK** and something unknown, and just below that is the signature:

———— *Francis Cutting* ————

By the early 1890's many changes were taking place in the canning industry. Companies were merging to form large corporations, can making was becoming automated, requiring less metal for each can and less solder to hold them together. Some of these cans found together under the one building were opened and eaten at the time of these changes. Some are hand made, while others were made by a machine.

The can below is another view of the **Cutting** Can where you are able to make out the word **JELLY** and **SAN FRANCISCO, CAL. U. S. A.**

The three letters **HES** indicate this can probably contained peaches. The printer was **DICKMAN JONES CO. S. F.**

The labels on the can pictured above and on the next page, along with the previous can, and the next can pictured, record a merger occurring at this time in history. The Cutting Company and the San Jose Fruit Packing Company had already joined forces. Now, The Cutting Company was absorbing the Colton Company.

This little bit of a label below created some excitement as I cleaned years of dirt and rust from it. It became apparent that the girl with the dog was the same one that was on the earlier Colton can (p.82), she had just gotten a little older. She is still carrying the fruit in her apron. The name on the cannery building behind her is no longer Colton, but Cutting. If the **Cutting** trademark was on the label, it was on an area that is missing. As noted, the illustration was still Colton's.

Cutting's trademark shown above appeared on the next label of the Cutting Packing Co., but the illustration contained a part from The San Jose Fruit Packing Company (California Fruits). They did retain the Colton name as a brand. The wonderful bear label was no longer in use (p. 14).

This was one of the mergers that eventually would become the California Fruit Canners Association, which was the result of a larger merger in 1899 that included eighteen old California companies.

On this early 1890's can the **Griffin** which at first covered one side of the label had shrunk considerably.

The Griffin was on the **Del Monte** brand in 1909, but gone by 1916.

This can ties the three companies just mentioned together. Through the rust you are able to read: **California Fruits,** and **PACKED BY CUTTING PACKING CO. SAN FRANCISCO, COLTON,** and possibly **SANTA ROSA.** The label was printed by **THE MON'L LABEL CO. BALTO. MD.**

The missing word is either **YELLOW** or **CLING.**

In just ten years the style of labels were taking on a different look, becoming more realistic and less artistic. By this time the word **STANDARD** had been adopted as the good grade of produce.

Except for these labels from the Cutting Packing Company and the Maryland Brand, the rest of the labels from the second find are the first ones of their represented companies.

Rust has nearly consumed some of these cans and labels but unless someone has some better preserved ones somewhere, this is the best there is. **THE UTAH CANNING CO.** of **OGDEN, UTAH,** was the first cannery between the Rocky Mountains and Western California. As a remembrance of their beginnings in Utah, and the fact that they were pioneering the

first canning operations in such a vast area, they used the name **PIONEER** Brand for their first canned product, **TOMATOES**. They also made their own cans during the winter.

They processed only 300 cans during their first year of operation in 1888. By 1890 they were paying farmers six dollars a ton for tomatoes, and women four cents a pail to peel them. A skilled worker could peel sixty pails in a ten hour day. Not a bad wage at that time.

There were two grades of tomatoes, 'Standards' for peeling; others for catsup, tomato juice, tomato sauce, etc.

The label is full of detail. Besides the cannery with houses, trees, fields and mountains in the background, there are parts of three trains, ten horses, five wagons, and eight people. The red and blue horses in the lower left corner are quite unique.

Out of all the labels found under structures, this is one of only three that I have seen even as a picture anywhere else. A picture of this label was in the personal collection of the owners of an antique shop in Ogden, Utah. It was a black and white picture of the label in an old history book, of Weber County, Utah. There was no date with the picture or in the book.

While researching the earlier cans I came across some history about the **WASATCH ORCHARD CO**. of **OGDEN, UTAH**. I wondered what would be the chances of finding one of their original labels. I could hardly believe it when I saw this can under the second building. The history could now be used.

In the early 1890's Jake Parker went to work in a cannery for $1.40 per day. Within thirty days he had been appointed company manager. Not long after this he devoted his

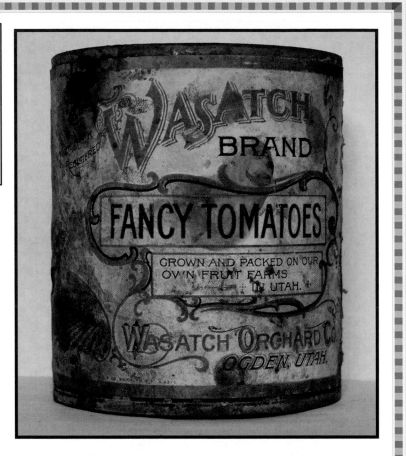

energies to get the freight rates that were discriminatory against the Utah canneries on an even plane. This made him popular with the canners but not with the railroads. Later while managing, among others, the Wasatch Company in West Ogden. Parker invested a large sum of money to construct a concrete loading platform. When the railroad engineers examined this new platform, at the peak of his canning season, they ordered it set back six inches farther from the cannery's side track before the railroad would deliver any more cars. The following morning he telephoned the railroad offices demanding that the engineers be promptly sent out to the Wasatch cannery to resurvey the platform and side track to correct an obvious error in calculations. A recheck was made in response to his demand.

There was ample clearance for all cars switched to the platform. The railroad apologized and empty cars rolled onto the track. The railroad never found out that his cannery workers during the night had moved the track several inches away from the platform, tamped down the ties and loose dirt, and covered up all evidence of their workmanship. It was much easier and quicker to move the track than take six inches off of a concrete platform.

The hole punched in the top was something that was done with every single can found under the boarding house. Any sealed product coming to two mile high Leadville will expand because of the lower air pressure. In canned goods it should be minimal, but maybe whoever opened it was afraid it might explode if they didn't poke a hole in it first.

Any package with air, like chips and marshmallows, will swell up considerably when brought up from a lower altitude.

The information printed on this label is significant in canning history. This is the first label to mention **machinery.** In 1886 all peas were shelled by hand. Inventers Bob Scott and the Chisholm brothers, Jack and C. P., joined forces, and by 1890 had combined a pea podder with a separator. This new machine would automatically separate peas from their pods and vines. They called it a pea VINER. This new machine could do the work of 600 hand workers. They leased their VINERS to canneries, and charged nine cents per dozen cans.

FRESH GREEN FLAVOR, GUARANTEED 30 MINUTES FROM FIELD TO CAN.
VINER PROCESS
CHAMPION EARLY JUNE PEAS

PACKED BY
CHISHOLM & SCOTT

THE VINER PROCESS
represents the highest ex——
automatic **machinery** insures——
CHAMPION BRAND
EARLY JUNE PEAS
[The missing words are likely]
excellence and **quality.**

These three labels are from the 1890's. The information printed on this unused label is worth noting. Chisholm and Scott claimed they processed their product within 30 minutes.

L. J. GALLANAN'S were a little more realistic. Their label says: '**This corn is brought from the field and packed in the can, in the least possible time, at Oneida, N. Y. for L. J. Gallanan.**'

This **ARMOUR CANNING CO.** label fell off the can shown on page 126. Other products listed on the can are called Celebrated Delicacies:

**IN TINS
BONED CHICKEN
POTTED CHICKEN
DEVILED CHICKEN
SLICED
STAR BACON**
—

**FOR SALE BY
ALL GROCERS.**

A less detailed label of another Brand from the **WASATCH ORCHARD CO.** of **OGDEN, UTAH.**

It was found at an antique shop in Philipsburg, Montana.

This label was never on a can.

Empson's
YE OLD FASHIONED
HOMINY
LIKE MOTHER USED TO MAKE

There were two of **Empson's HOMINY** cans under the building. It required both to know what was being canned and by whom. The illustration is quite interesting. You have a woman stirring a kettle hanging over an open fire. Next to the fire is a barrel with liquid running from a spigot into a pan on the ground.

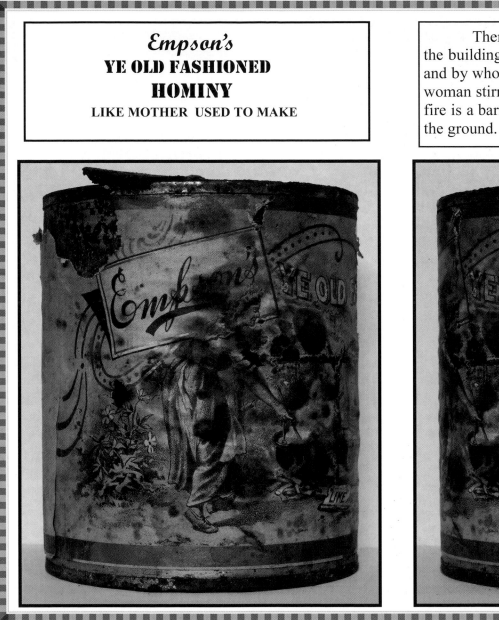

The back of the label, although quite rusted, tells us where and by whom it was canned.

**THE EMPSON
PACKING Co.
LONGMONT, COLO.**

When one segment of history merges with another segment it not only makes it more interesting, it also makes the time period that is being recorded more identifiable.

About a year after the 'first cans' were tossed under the log home during construction, Doc Holliday arrived in Leadville. About this same time John Empson, accompanied by his daughter arrived in Denver. Ironically Holliday and Empson came to Colorado for a common reason. They both suffered from lung problems and needed a drier climate if they hoped to live much longer.

Doc Holliday only changed his location, but not his lifestyle, and after his last shootout he moved to Glenwood Springs, Colorado, where he died in 1887.

John Empson returned to Cincinnati, Ohio, where he had made and sold candy, to finalize his move to Colorado in 1886. By 1887 he had opened in Longmont his first J. Empson & Daughter's cannery. Including his 'Daughter' in the name during a time period when few women were involved in industry proved a boom for advertising their business.

In 1890 after their first successful year in canning, a fire destroyed the cannery, warehouse, and contents. A year later they had rebuilt their plant and were expanding. They canned a wide range of products including asparagus, tomatoes, hominy, and pumpkin, but his favored product was currant jelly.

Many experts of that time declared copper kettles unsafe for cooking currants, therefore Empson had 4000 silver dollars melted down and made into a four foot diameter silver kettle. He had engraved on the outside his company name with 'Daughter' included. He toured the country with his silver kettle and created a tremendous market for his currant jelly. It's not known whether he ever actually used it to cook his jelly. Most of the silver in the dollars he used likely came from Leadville.

In 1890 he planted 150 acres of peas, which was a large field for that time before machinery was extensively used in harvesting and canning produce. That same year Chisholm & Scott had successfully tested their pea viner at Springville, New York. Empson sent them a telegram ordering two of the viners, each being about the size of a railroad boxcar, for his plant. The next year he planted 300 acres of peas and ordered two more viners. He required Jack Chisholm to give them his personal service until the canning season was over.

The next year when Chisholm returned he saw that the competitive Empson had started manufacturing his own viners. Empson now began leasing his viners to any reliable canner for a royalty of three cents for a dozen cans. Lawsuits ensued that lasted years, with the only winners being the lawyers and the canneries, who now paid only three cents a dozen for the use of the viners. Empson eventually lost the lawsuit, but paid very little in damages.

During this same time period he employed Luther Burbank, known for his seed research, to experiment with new strains of peas. Burbank's name appeared for many years on Empson's labels.

Empson's plant was considered the largest pea cannery in the world. He also was known for his own periodical, **The Pea Pod.**

He died in 1926, and the next year the old Empson properties were reorganized with the Kuner Pickle Company.

Below:
All that is left of **Empson's 'DAISY PEAS'** label.
Just below the **S** on **PEAS** it is printed, DESIGN REGISTERED. Most of the wording is missing, but you can decipher **COLORADO.** On the lower right it tells it's **PACKED BY THE EMPSON CO.** GARDENS AND PACKING HOUSE IN LONGMONT, COLO.

From my research, The **KUNER PICKLE CO.**, started in 1883 at Greeley. This would make them the first name in canning in Colorado. They moved to Brighton in 1895 and in 1916 merged with the Empson Company.

These remnants of labels on this page are all that remained of Kuner's history from under the boarding house. The can on the right is **SAUER KRAUT.** The information at the top says**:**

This SAUER KRAUT is prepared and cooked with great care, and will be found a delicious addition to the line of TABLE DELICACIES. It does away entirely with the odor so objectionable to many when cooked at home. The location at the bottom is **DENVER, COLO.**

The other side said: **KUNER'S HOME COOKED SAUER KRAUT.**

The two pieces of labels shown together here survived their cans and are the only **TOMATOES** label that displays a green tomato. The information given after **TO-MATOES** says: **Every Can full of Meat.** Which means the tomatoes are in chunks.

The label was printed by the **WESTERN LITHO. CO. DENVER.**

Six cans of this brand of peas were found, but they were so far gone that four of them were sacrificed to reconstruct this one label. All that was left of one of the labels was the young woman's face, which was missing on the other five.

QUEEN OF THE WEST
ATLANTIC PACKING Co
ATLANTIC, IOWA
EARLY JUNE PEAS

118

The label below was about gone, but it was the only one that still had the paper that contained the bigger brand name **QUEEN OF THE WEST** and the tops of the peas. This was the only label found that had a Native American illustration.

The label above is the pieced together one.

Atlantic, Iowa was a stop on the Rock Island Railroad. A house located in this area was used in the 1850's as a stop on the Underground Railroad for runaway slaves.
I could find nothing about this cannery.

In January of 2005 I was back under the old boarding house for a more detailed search of the debris. The partial label on the left was found. At first I thought it would fit the can on the right. Upon closer examination I realized the lettering at the bottom was different.

Instead of **A. BOOTH & COMPANY**, it reads **A. BOOTH PACKING CO**. The picture is the same, only faded. Both were discarded at about the same time. From the information below, the one on the left is likely the older of the two.

On May 1,1890, the **A. Booth Packing Co.** registered their trademark as: 'A series of panels, the said panels comprising circular figures, in color, on a ground of contrasting color, the panels being separated by ribbon-like bands of a color contrasting from those of the panel.' On September 15, 1891, the second use of the word **contrasting** was changed to **different.**

SELECT PINEAPPLE
The cannery buildings have smoke spewing from the chimneys (at the time a sign of production). A train is seen clearly in the piece on the left, also horses pulling wagons.

A. BOOTH & COMPANY

GOOD SEAL

Over ten years before Jim Dole started canning pineapples in Hawaii, A. Booth was canning them in Baltimore. They were shipped up from Florida or the West Indies where pineapples were grown at this time in history.

EYELESS AND

CORELESS

SELECT PINEAPPLE

You can see the band connecting the panels. They weren't contrasting, only different, which places this can after 1891.

PACKED AT

BALTIMORE, MD. U. S. A.

A. BOOTH

AND

COMPANY

The deteriorated label below was the key to finding the history of the entire group of cans found under the building in 2004. After studying all of the cans and labels retrieved, it was realized that not a one had a date. No newspaper or anything else found was dated. One can was tightly wedged inside another can that was wrapped in paper with no label. Upon closer examination, paper was noticed between the two cans. With needle nose pliers I was able to twist the rusted inside can to make it smaller and pull it out. The paper inside was this label, and it had a date!

This label reads:
STRIKE CAN ON THE TOP ALL AROUND THE EDGE UNTIL OPENED.
A STONE OR A STOVE LID LIFTER WILL DO AS WELL AS A HAMMER.
PAT. JAN 12, 1892.
EUREKA CAN OPENING Co. NEW YORK.

PACKED BY
ANDERSON PRESERVING CO.
CAMDEN, N. J.

Below is all that's left of the can that was twisted from inside the other can. It is also the one that was struck until opened. I don't know how long they made this type of can, but it couldn't have been very tidy. It sounds as if it should have been the first 'Don't try this at home ad.'

Seeing the condition of this can makes the survival of the label even more remarkable.

In the 1870's Anderson was in partnership with Campbell, the same one who later concentrated on soup.

Ever since the discovery of the first pile of cans, it has been a continuing search for more old cans and labels, with the hope of locating any additional historical information to increase our own knowledge and collection. Generally the outcome has been quite lacking. Finally in desperation we went walking outside Leadville in the sagebrush to see how cans survive when laying exposed on the ground. Labels don't survive at all, but in a dry climate some cans remain for many years. A few interesting cans were found.

The two small cans above were machine made, and designed to be opened with a key. Both were opened with a can opener instead.

On the inside of the cans there is a weakening line where the key would peel it open. The smallest can could have been Underwood Deviled Ham. Finding these reminded us of what discarded tin cans are supposed to look like.

The smell of wet sagebrush after a summer rain brought back wonderful memories of mountain camping, and eating from a tin can.

This is an example of hauling something home without any real reason for doing so. All I remember is when I found it under a house it caught my attention because of the embossed letters. It was so rusty and dirty they weren't even readable. After an attempt at cleaning you could read the end that says, **OPEN HERE WITH PENKNIFE.**

It was opened with some kind of knife, but not at the right section. There was a reason for the instructions.

On January 12, 1892, three patents were issued relating to cans. One of these had to do with the deliberate weakening of a strip on one end to make them easier to open.

Ever since the first tin canister was soldered together around 1810, inventors have been trying to figure out a better way to extract the contents out of them. The first containers were recommended to be, 'cut around close to the edge with a hammer and chisel' (You can imagine where your food would go). Forty-eight years later Ezra Warner invented a can opener that looked like a bayonet. These were not even sold to the public but were used at the store where you bought the canned goods. Unless you were going to eat the food immediately it was up to each individual to figure out how to open the can.

During the Civil War soldiers used their bayonets to open the cans. In the 1870's a wheeled can opener was invented. If the cans we found are any indication of reality in the mining towns, the can opener wasn't the first item on your list of essential possessions.

Of the over two hundred cans found on the two occasions, one may have been opened with a can opener. The rest were like this example, cut with a knife wherever you wanted, and only as much as necessary to pry open the lid and extract the food.

During the process of writing I would place a can in front of me to be able to record the information from the can and label. Only then did I realize this oyster can on the right from **BALTIMORE** said **A. BOOTH CO.**, the same company that canned the strawberries and pineapple. Seeing how the can was soldered together and knowing the A. Booth Co. was registering their labels by 1890, this cans age fits into the early 1890's.

Another invention at this time period was for the keyed can. Finally you could open a can without some sort of tool. Processed meats were especially suited for this type of design. After finding these early keyed cans my first thoughts were that they would all have contained meat products. Within a short period of time enough other cans were found to know they at least tried other products with keyed openers.

The keys on these keyed cans could well be among the first ever used. They are stamped like the old square nails rather than round, although the round key on the right could be nearly as old. It was around 1890 that round wire began to be produced, and the round key would be made the same way.

The round key could be mass produced cheaper and quicker, therefore the square key probably didn't last very long.

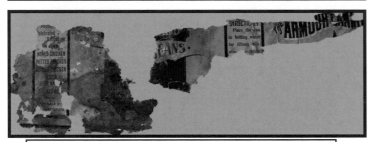

(Above) Remaining label from the can below.

The label above from the **ARMOUR PACKING CO.**, of **KANSAS CITY, U. S. A.,** contained **VEAL LOAF.** The red lettering says **HELMET BRAND** and **DELICATELY PREPARED.** The oval has a helmet and shoulders of armor.

On the left is another **ARMOUR** can found with the second cans and it has a square key. Part of its label was wrapped up with the key. The can was in such bad shape the label fell off. It contained Pork and Beans or Baked Beans, which either didn't contain much liquid or was rather messy when opened. (More details on page 113.)

Philip D. Armour opened a hog packing plant in Milwaukee in 1860. By 1871 Armour had a plant in Kansas City.

The blue can on the right with the lettering printed directly on the metal is another example of a non-meat product in a keyed can. It contained pudding. It was found in an unprotected area laying in the sagebrush. It's probably from the 1940's.

Coffee cans and 'Spam' also made good use of the keyed can.

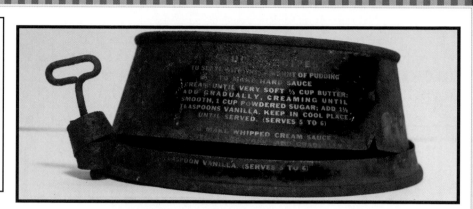

I picked up the can on the lower left because it reminded me of the sardine cans seen in old cartoons that mice would have for beds. The key peeled the lid back to get access to the product. It wasn't sardines. The bottom of the can is stamped **Kippered Herring**. This design eliminated spillage of liquids.

The rusted piece below was found at an old mine dump. It was connected to its other end until picked up. It then fell apart. It's the larger end of a **Libby's** hand soldered can found in the condition we would expect, in a dry climate, for its age.

127

These two rusty cans came from under another house in Leadville. The one below says **BALTIMORE OYSTERS PACKED FOR T. T. CORNFORTH DENVER, COLORADO.** The back has a shield, and **SHIELD BRAND.**

This can reads: **ELLIS AND FLINT PACKERS DENVER, COLO.** At least the one below, if not both, probably had the oysters shipped to Denver from Baltimore in bulk, and then packed in these cans.

Steel wool was used to make it readable, which is not recommended for anything of value.

After finding the first cans with labels, we began looking everywhere we could think of to see how common or rare they might be. It was over a year of searching before this taped together label on its original can was found at an antique mall in Denver. We knew it was old because of the graphics, no weight on the label, and a hand soldered can.

While researching the original labels I kept watching for anything about this brand. It was not until I saw the date 1892 on the Anderson label, in the second find, that I began looking for trademarks from the late 1880's and early 1890's.

We now were able to know the history on three cans found at different locations. The oyster, pineapple, and strawberry cans.

STRAWBERRIES
OVAL
TRADEMARK
BRAND
A. BOOTH & CO.
BALTIMORE, MD. U. S. A.
The printer was the
CRUMP FIVE COLOR LABEL PRESS
N. Y.
This label has a number:
B1354

Several salmon cans were found among the 1890's cans, but only this one still had a label that was readable. Its label is quite unique.

GOLDEN RULE
BRAND
SALMON

The earlier labels could be cleaned very carefully with a Q-Tip, mild soap and water. By sacrificing a duplicate of one of these later labels, it was realized that the ink would come off with the most delicate of cleaning.

Sadly, from an historical viewpoint, the labels and cans had become more bio-degradable.

The middle of the salmon is missing, but for lying under this old boarding house for close to 110 years, it's not in too bad of condition.

The rulers and measuring tapes on the label are accurate. By these rulers alone you are able to know that the distance around the can is nine and a quarter inches, and it's four and one half inches tall.

J. P. HALLER
MANAGER.
SAN FRANCISCO, CAL.

It was printed by
SCHMIDT LABEL & LITH CO S. F.

In the early 1890's **SARDINES** were still being imported from France. This can was among the first keyed cans ever made. It's a little hard to see but the picture shows two hands demonstrating how to hold the can with one hand and turn the key with the other. Both sardine can labels were printed directly on the cans.

The small can holding the sardine can is machine made. The sardine can is hand soldered. They were found together.

The eye in the triangle below is probably the trademark for this can.

All that is left of the label, to the right, identifies it as **EXTRA QUALITY TOMATOES** and that it was printed by the **U.S.P. CO. BKLN. N.Y.W-1848.** I hoped this was a date, but it appears to be just the label number. The United States Printing Co. was not in business in 1848.

What I had written above was all I knew until the more extensive search in 2005. During that search I found the piece below that joined perfectly with the **WO** (bottom right) and solved the mystery of where the tomatoes came from. **WOODS CROSS, UTAH** is about ten miles north of Salt Lake City.

Maybe, somewhere out there, someone has a complete one of this beautiful and colorful label.

Three different **EVAPORATED CREAM** cans from under the old boarding house.

One is from **ST. CHARLES, ILLINOIS. U. S. A.**

The **SUNSET BRAND** from the **AMERICAN CONDENSED MILK CO.** is from **SAN FRANCISCO.**

The one with **Lady Liberty** is unknown. I couldn't find any Unsweetened Cream Brand that ended in **an.**

Lady Liberty is holding a globe in the talons of an eagle in her right hand, and a torch in her left.

This is the top of the **SUNSET BRAND** can shown in the center of the previous page. Around the rim it reads: **TO OPEN THE CAN PUNCH ON THE STARS, SHAKE WELL BEFORE OPENING.** The center reads: **SUNSET CREAM, PERFECTLY STERILIZED, ANSWERS FULLY ANY OF THE PURPOSES OF RAW MILK OR CREAM. CONTAINS ONLY ELEMENTS SUPPLIED BY THE COW. ECONOMICAL & DELICIOUS.**

The **ROSE BRAND** on the right gives enough information to tie it in with the earlier labels. The **ANGLO SWISS CONDENSED MILK CO.** of **NEW YORK** , and Switzerland, was the company where John Meyenberg conducted his experiments for sugarless evaporated milk. In 1902 Borden's took over all the Anglo–Swiss American holdings. In 1905 the Anglo-Swiss company of Europe merged with the Henri Nestle Company.

The label on the right doesn't give enough information to accurately identify much about it. At one time the fruits had been beautiful. You can make out **& CRESCENT**, and **AM** at the bottom. This may have been **JAM.** The larger letters are probably the last four letters of **CALIFORNIA**.

Sac City received its name in 1855 for the Native Americans of the area. The only history I could find concerning this label comes from the label itself, and a map of Iowa.

Sac City is located some eighty miles east of Sioux City, Iowa, on the North Raccoon River. Coon Valley is mentioned in history around 1879. **COON VALLEY CORN** would have gotten its name from this source.

This can and label made it to Western Montana, where it was purchased in 2004 at the town of Philipsburg.

The characteristics of the **COON VALLEY CORN** label are similar to the other 1890's labels, but it could date from the 1880's.

136

This label is the **POPULAR BRAND**. The can contained **STRING BEANS**. The other information reads:
EXTRA QUALITY
PACKED BY
W. M. FAIT COMPANY
Baltimore, Md.

The label is of a girl holding a can with her holding the same can in her right hand. There is also an artist, wearing nothing but a hat, painting the graphics. This was with the second find, and is hand soldered.

A variation of this label is in the book 'The Art of the Label' by Robert Opie.

H. O. WILBUR & SON'S
of Philadelphia introduced the Stirring Cupid in 1887.

This can was machine made and contained no solder. Their trademark is the little winged cupid with his bow and arrows stirring a cup of cocoa.

It was found in an antique store.

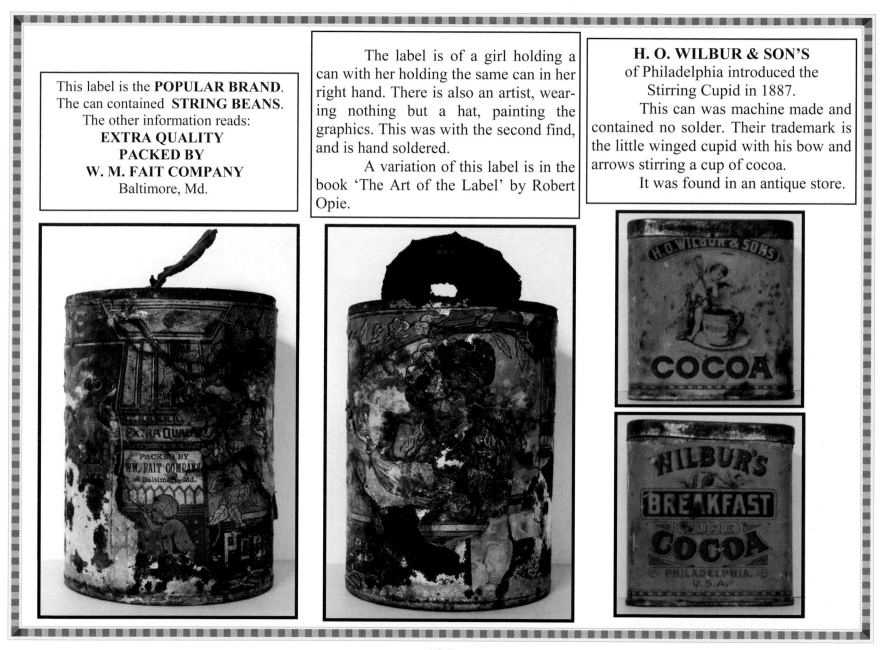

I had hoped to find some more pieces of this label to identify where it came from, but all that was found was the piece on the opposite page (center) that shows the peas in the tureen.

The lettering of **COLUMBINE** is the same as the **COLUMBINE MILK CO**. of Denver that I remember from the 50's. I haven't been able to find a connection.

These labels date from the 1890's. This can contained some kind of **BEANS**. The picture resembles Lima beans.

The Columbine gives the indication it is a Colorado Brand, since the Columbine is the State Flower.

Both sides are shown below.

The can below found among the 1890's cans is a good example of a bad use of solder on an early can. Like any new product or industry you hope the 'bugs' get worked out before too much damage is done. Many years were required to completely phase out hand soldering. (Over 100 years).

Edwin Norton, a pioneer in making cans with machinery, acquired some 5000 patents in his years of making a better tin can. In 1901 the Norton Tin Can & Plate Company merged with over one hundred other companies to form the American Can Company.

A sampling of pieces of labels that give additional clues in the history of early advertising. The **BLACK-BERRY** piece from 1882 highlights the difference ten years made in the style of design on the 1890's labels. The fancy graphics were for the most part gone on the 1890's labels.

The pieces of **SAUERKRAUT** labels from the **KUNER PICKLE CO.**, reveal that the label was changed twice in the short time the cans were tossed under the boarding house. The faded piece retained the letters **NVER** that identified the location as **DENVER**.

The piece with the

is **Star Brand PORK AND BEANS with tomato sauce,** from the **ARMOUR CAN-NING CO.**, of **CHICAGO**.

The second search under the old boarding house was in the hope of filling in a few of the missing pieces in the history of the cans retrieved in October of 2004.

Several labels received missing pieces, and enough new pieces were found to know there is a wide variety of beautiful labels that hopefully will in time be found.

Before refrigeration, rapid transportation, floating canneries, and giant corporations, nearly every town with a fishing fleet had a cannery. To set your product apart, names and images would be used to catch the consumers attention. This is an example of a salmon label designed to make you look twice although the young woman and the name had little or nothing to do with the product.

This label was an unused one purchased at an antique mall for $35. It is a little taller but fits on the older salmon cans.

The can below was the only one found under the boarding house that wasn't badly rusted. It was a hand soldered can used for salmon, that outlasted its label. It is a good example of how the lacquer preserved the can from rust. The hole punched in the top can be seen. None of the earlier cans had the hole.

The first salmon cans were painted with a mixture of red lead, turpentine, and linseed oil. Fiery red cans meant red salmon. That explains why the early paper salmon labels were primarily red.

This label is from the 1890's. It is an old label on a newer can, and was found in an antique shop. On this side the printing at the top reads:

SLAUGHTERED AND PACKED ON THE RANGE.

Above the **R** of the word **RANGE** is printed:
PITTSBURGH LABEL Co.

FORT McKAVETT, TEXAS is an Historical Site today.

GUARANTEED
TO KEEP
IN ANY CLIMATE
DIRECTIONS.
OPEN AT TOP
With ordinary can opener. If desired hot, place the can in boiling water twenty minutes before opening. Season to suit the taste
FIRST QUALITY.

As mentioned on page 2, it was a label similar to this that Mr. Kovel held up as the oldest he had seen. At first I thought the labels were alike, until comparing this label with the one on page 106 of the Kovel's book, 'THE LABEL MADE ME BUY IT.' The size of the panels are different, much of the lettering is different, and this one gives the printers name. The stripes going around the can are also different. Some of the lettering on this label appears to be an older style.

These three labels are an example of the changes that occur in a trademark. The basic design is the same. but the artwork tries not to appear old fashioned. If these labels are consistent with the older ones we found the fancier one on the left would be the oldest. Most labels tended to simplify instead of getting fancier. The two on the left are from the 1890's. The one on the right is after 1906.

These labels survived in boxes in warehouses where they were discovered in recent years and put on the market. They were extras that were never used. Many of them are quite beautiful, and where available can be purchased at a cost between five and fifty dollars, depending on rarity. These labels are old enough that they don't fit modern cans, but they fit perfectly on the pre-1882 cans that were missing labels.

This is the second of the two cans purchased on eBay. It's not as old as any of the cans we found under the structures because the weight is given (1 lb. 3 oz.), which usually means it's after 1906, but there are exceptions. It's still old enough to have some extra graphics.

Dark blue backgrounds were also missing among the first cans, making this a welcome addition.

Searching antique shops and shows for old labels on the original cans doesn't yield many results.

In five years' time we have bought only nine cans with their original labels. Three of them are pre-1900.

The portrait of Washington on this label, for the **Mt. Vernon, Washington, Cream Co.,** is certainly an appropriate design from this location.

The word **weight** is an indication that this label is after 1906. The soldered pin hole in the top dates it earlier than the mid-twenties.

This can was found at a shop in Ferndale, Washington.

An early design of the Olympic Canning Co.

This style of design still retains the characteristics of some of the 1890 labels, but it probably dates from the 1930's. It is the same style of can that was used by the Stella Brand.

The Olympic Canning Co. ceased operations in 1959.

As mentioned earlier very few old labeled cans have been saved. They turn up in various antique shops now and again. This is the most recent one we found, in January of 2005.

This can had a hole poked in the top like all of the ones I had found from the 1890's.

The collection of tops below began with finding the one in front in the hollow space of a lath and plaster wall.

RED-TOP is a popular name used for a wide variety of products. In these few pages there is **RED-TOP SYRUP** and Red Top Whiskey. We have a gunny sack for Red Top Potatoes, and a one and a quarter ounce canister of **PEARSON'S RED TOP SNUFF**. This is an example of a possible collection of a name that would be endless.

Another use of the word red in a name, used for a different type of top, is **RED TOP FLOUR** on the next page. On the enlarged map of the mining claims on page 50, in the upper right hand corner, is the claim 'Red Headed Mary.'

146

These are rare, early, highly collectable, one cup flour and sugar scoops used for advertising.

This collection began with the finding of the one on the right, under some unknown powder (possibly powdered soap), in an old heavy paper barrel.

We have only found these four.

To the right of his foot, on the edge, reads **ONE STANDARD CUP**.

The automation of tin can making meant the elimination of many jobs for tinsmiths, but for the skilled tinsmith many other containers continued to be made. This collection of sewing machine and bicycle oil cans began with finding the first one inside a wall.

The one pint creamer and the canteen below are hand made and bear the brass label of the **WESTERN HARDWARE CO., LEADVILLE, COLO.** All are prized collectables.

TOWLE'S LOG CABIN SYRUP was patented on April 20, 1897. The first three Log Cabin label designs were paper. It was not until 1919 that they changed from paper to lithographed tin.

This tin was found under another house, along with other items dating from the late 1920's. This was before the old labeled can discovery. At this time, if someone showed much interest in an item I had found, I would sell it in my wife Cherie's antique shop, sometimes over her protests.

This is the back of the can, the front was in the dirt and is completely gone. The main difference in this view from the first design is the **NET CONTENTS, 1 PINT 10 OZ. FL.** instead of **2 1/4 pounds net weight.** Under the net contents it reads: **COPYRIGHTED 1914 BY THE TOWLE MAPLE PRODUCTS CO.**, and the tiny letters at the bottom right, **A. C. CO. 82-A-01.**

A. C. CO. is the American Can Company, which was created in 1901 by the amalgamation of many can manufacturing companies.

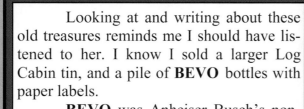

Looking at and writing about these old treasures reminds me I should have listened to her. I know I sold a larger Log Cabin tin, and a pile of **BEVO** bottles with paper labels.

BEVO was Anheiser Busch's non-alcoholic drink made during prohibition.

This tin was the second lithographed design of **LOG CABIN SYRUP** dating from the late 1920's.

A **LOG CABIN** advertising spoon that pre-dates the can. The back is embossed **PAT. Jan. 14, 08. TOWLE; ST. PAUL, U. S. A.**

Thousands of ink bottles have been uncovered over the years. This speaks well for the literacy rate of those who rushed to Leadville and their desire to keep in touch with family. The three bottles below were found discarded with the oldest cans, indicating the workers spent part of their time writing. The one on the left is Carter, Dinsmore & Co. Their trademark #6,192 for Writing Ink was registered on June 11, 1878.

The Eagle Pencil Co. of New York was registering trademarks for lead pencils in 1878 and 1879. Writing Paper was also registered during these years.

The pickle bottle on the right, from the **GLOBE PICKLE Co.**, of **ST. LOUIS & CHICAGO**, was also with the oldest cache of cans. The words in the globe are **OUR OWN**.

Photo: Bill Sagstetter

This photo gives us two examples of history in America in the 1870's. The structure shows us how the first buildings in the mining areas of the West were constructed. The lumber was rough cut native pine, one inch thick, and anywhere between six and eighteen inches wide. Even today, many of the original outbuildings on the alleys have this look.

The sign is as unique as the town. The green and yellow **JOHN DEERE** logo is one of the most recognized trademarks in the world today. I have found no history of a yellow, black and red sign. The deer leaping over a log is the same one that was registered on February 22, 1876, for 'plows and cultivators.'

The sign itself is enameled metal and does not have the word **TRADEMARK** on the log, or **MOLINE ILL.** under it. This sign could be older than 1876, and if it is, Leadville is one place it would be preserved, as the cans and labels were.

The first deer used in this trademark was an African deer. It wasn't until 1950 that the deer was changed to the American White Tail with the antlers facing forward.

John Deere is credited with making the first steel plow in 1837. He was a blacksmith and forged it from an old saw blade.

A cast iron plow was patented in 1797.

Without an efficient plow, large farms for supplying canneries with produce could not have happened.

An attractive and informative label from the Quaker Oats Company. Another example of the use of the grizzly in advertising.

The Quaker man was registered on September 4, 1877.

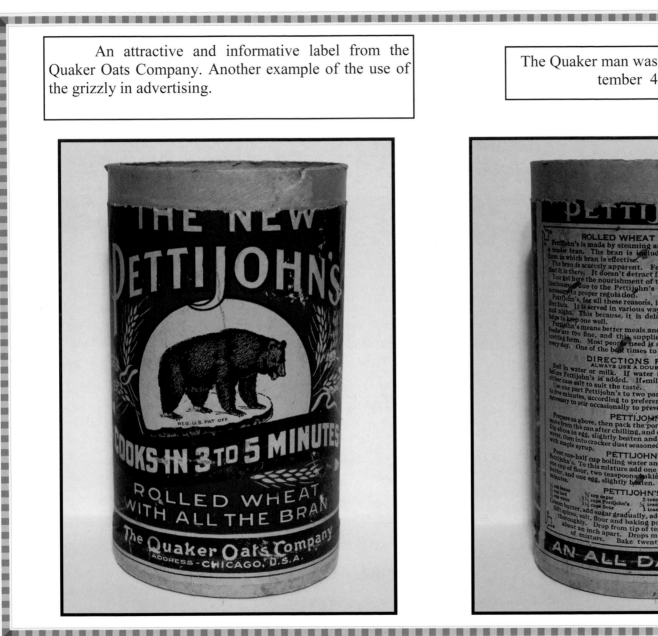

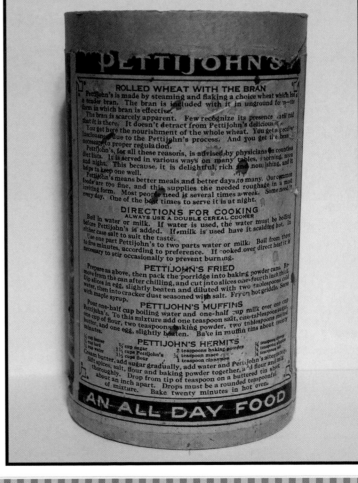

Early advertising for the
Pettijohn's Brand
From **SCRIBNER'S MAGAZINE ADVERTISER**.
The sign on the wall reads:——>

PETTIJOHN'S
"BEAR" IN MIND
OUR
TRADE MARK
Breakfast Food
FEEDS THE BODY AND THE BRAIN

If children living in the teens and twenties of the last century were like all we have known, they would have cut the bear off the container even if they never sent for the offer.

An offer at the bottom of this ad on the right gives one reason why only a few of the containers on the previous page survived.

Free   Free
MOTHER GOOSE IN PROSE
BY L. FRANK BAUM.
Send Three Bears cut from Pettijohn's Breakfast Food package, and 8 cents in stamps to pay for mailing, and we will send you free a copy of the first part of MOTHER GOOSE IN PROSE.

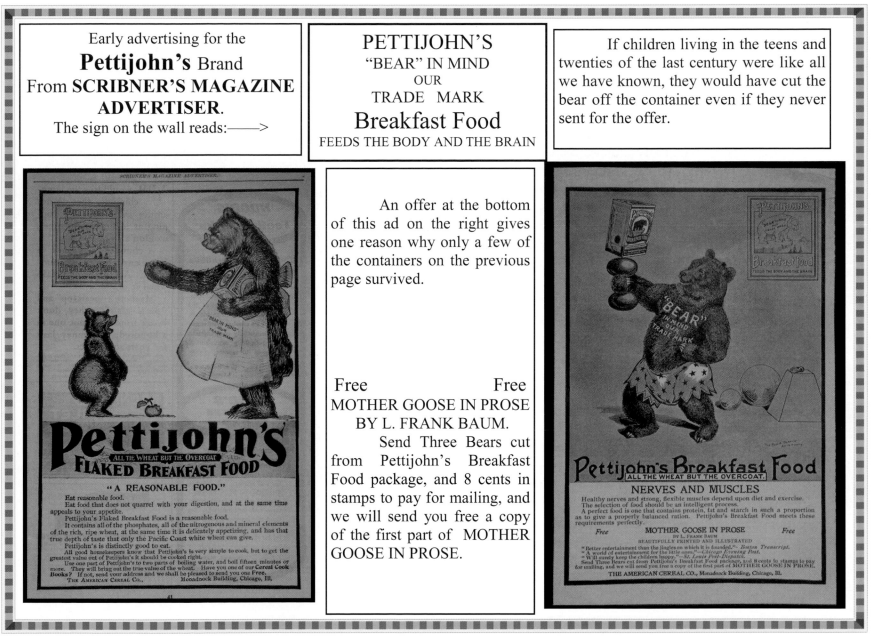

153

SHARDS AND OTHER DISCARDS

Archeologists have long found the histories of ancient civilizations in there rubbish heaps and city dumps. After the invention of the printing press, and the successful printing of 'The Guttenberg Bible' between 1450 and 1455, a greater amount of history began to be recorded, and the groundwork was laid that would eventually include colored labels. Today we still are able to find fascinating unrecorded history wherever man has lived by the things he threw away.

No matter where you walk today you see the results of people discarding things. In most cases it is unsightly and disturbing, but when you find things that were discarded more than a hundred years ago they take on a different light.

After this much time has passed most of the unsightly things are long gone, and only the most durable items remain. For the most part the majority of what's left is still just trash, but now and again something you feel is worth picking up catches your eye.

An area long known to those searching for 'treasure' are the old outhouses. It appears that in most homes drinking in the house was not acceptable, so those inclined to drink would take a bottle to the outhouse and when finished they dropped the empty 'evidence' down the hole. These and countless other items met a similar fate. One hundred years later, more or less, the undesirables in most cases have turned back into something less undesirable. The glass, pottery and some metal items remain. Many of the old drug store, beer and whiskey bottles found in antique shops today, came from this source.

The majority of these areas by now have either been dug up or built over.

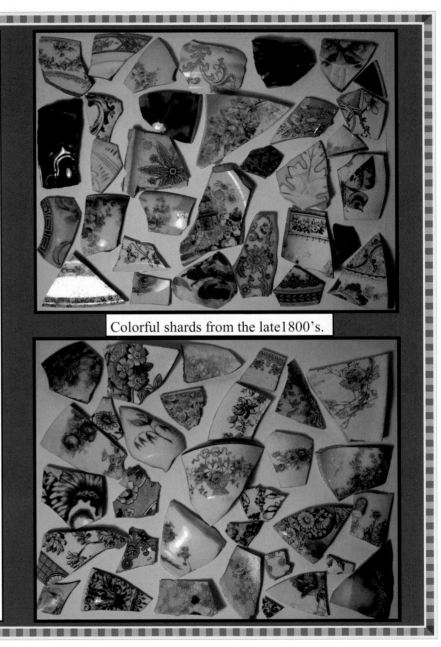

Colorful shards from the late1800's.

154

Below is a sampling of the marbles lost by their original owners, and found over the years under houses, in vacant lots, yards and alleys in the Leadville area. The playing of various games with marbles has entertained children and families for decades. Today marbles are highly collectable. The majority of these shown date from the late 1800's.

Below are a few of the hundreds of glass and shell buttons that are uncovered continually by rain, snow and wind. The buttons are all that remain of the discarded clothing of years gone by.

Tiny, lost and discarded doll parts and pendants, we also picked up, are scattered among the buttons.

The tiny three hole buttons on the cover of the book are from discarded baby clothes.

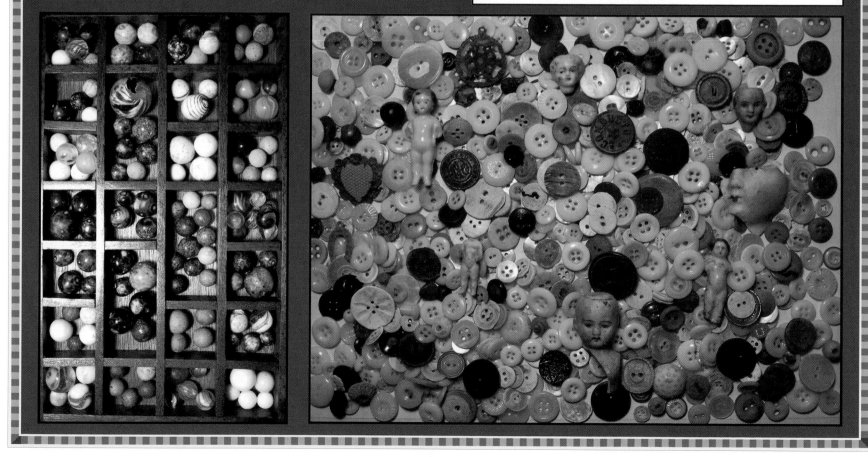

Dumps or landfills around boomtowns have proved to be a virtual treasure trove of artifacts. The old Leadville dump was in operation from 1879 until about 1959.

With the population exceeding 35,000 people in the early 1880's, you can imagine the amount of objects discarded over this eighty-year time span.

People have always scavenged from dumps, even when they were in operation; but once they close, if allowed, people start digging them back up.

My first experience with the Leadville dump must have been about 1965 while employed by the Telephone Company. We were burying a cable, plowed in by a 'Bull Dozer' that unearthed old bottles, which were promptly picked up by a local resident whose husband was digging and sifting an area of the older part of the dump. My curiosity was aroused, but not seriously, as to what could be that interesting at an old dump. Time and circumstances have turned that curiosity into an enjoyable journey into the past.

While in operation, burning was constant at this old dump, eliminating combustible materials, melting glass and distorting metals. What is remarkable is how much remained to be found in later years.

After being thrown away, burned, buried, run over by heavy equipment, dug up by hand and backhoe, sifted, walked over with metal detectors, dug up again by organized bottle digging groups and individuals, it is still, as of 2004, an area that yields an occasional treasure. Just walking across the area, scanning the ground for items washed clean by rain, kicked out by ground squirrels, or the hooves of elk or deer, brings back history. These pages contain a few of the broken and worn items that still stir one's imagination. Over the years different people would lease or own sections of this dump, and countless collections have been obtained. Thousands of bottles, children's dishes, whiskey jugs, coins and tokens have come from this source. Close to twenty gold coins, that were seen by more than the persons who found them, have been located. Some were likely in unchecked clothing that was discarded; but the greater number were probably hidden in some piece of furniture that was later thrown away. Many of these items have made their way into books. Most of this area is now private property.

The items pictured on the following pages are some of the leftovers, after the really great collections had already been gathered.

A thin copper alloy spoon found laying on the ground near the old dump. It's inscribed **LOWNEY**.

If you can see old buttons laying around, you know there are still other things to be found.

By using the bottoms of discarded Ironstone China as a gauge, we learned that most of it was imported from England during the 1880's.

In these few shards found, East Liverpool, Austria, Holland and France are also represented. The Lion and Unicorn are the most common.

The oyster and scallop shells found scattered all over the old dump area have survived in some cases for well over 100 years.

The amount of shells seen, reveals that the vast majority of seafood came to Leadville in barrels instead of cans. This may explain why only one oyster can was found.

****

These are the same kind of shells that were used to manufacture the old shell buttons.

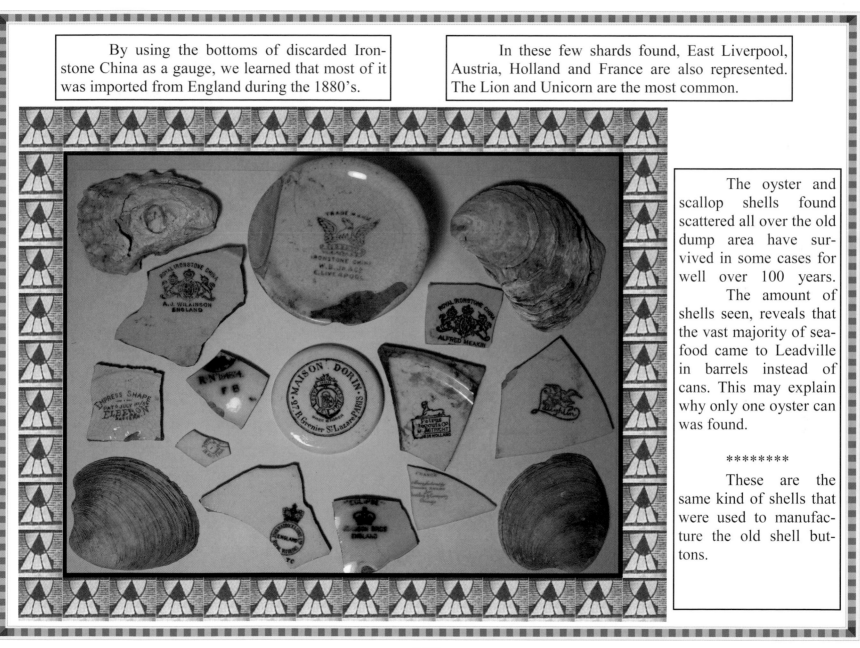

157

This is one of the two Budweiser beer bottles found with the cans. Their history is tied into the same time period as the can labels. I have seen much better examples of this label, but those examples weren't found in the dirt.

The label #1790 for Budweiser Lager Beer was issued to C. Conrad & Co. on December 3, 1878.

The lower part of the label is written in German.

The black on the inside of the bottle is what's left of 122 year old dried up beer.

Below is the **CCCo.** Trademark embossed on the bottom of the bottle.

An early advertisement for their beer is seen on the side of The Tabor Opera House in the old photo on page 98.

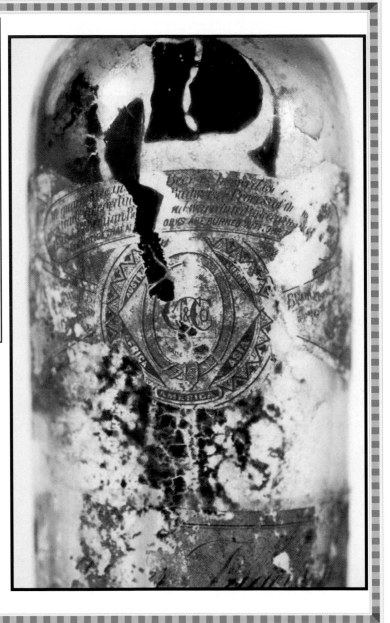

Various **CITRATE** of **MAGNE-SIA** bottles are dug from the ground in abundance. The contents made the after effects of certain foods endurable. This one had a unique stopper. I was surprised by the recommended dosage found embossed on this bottle.
DOSE-ADULTS ONE HALF TO ONE BOTTLE AS DESIRED CHILDREN IN PROPORTION TO AGE.

These two embossed **BUDWEISER** bottles are the same in their wording, but the words are different in size and shape. This is another example of how fast labels were changed.

Both bottles say **PATENT No. 6376,** which in reality was the number of their registered trademark.

On July 16, 1878, Trademark **#6376** for **LA-GER BEER** was registered to **C. Conrad & Co.** of St. Louis Mo., and Germany. The trademark was the word **BUDWEISER** and the character **CCCo.**

Both appear to have had a paper label over the embossed letters.

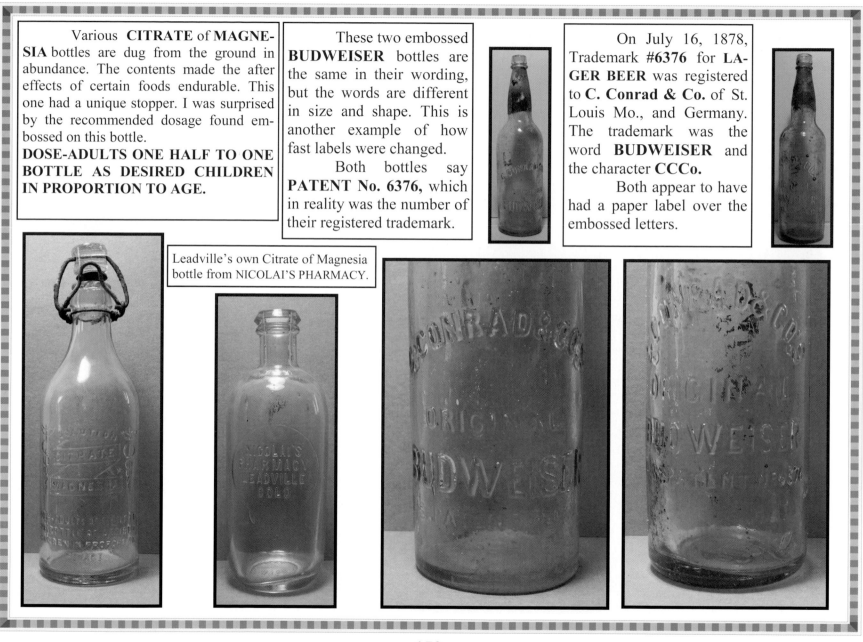

Leadville's own Citrate of Magnesia bottle from NICOLAI'S PHARMACY.

Below are various stoppers from pre-1900's bottles.

Included are perfume, chemical, whiskey, Lea & Perrins Worcestershire Sauce, and Citrate of Magnesia.

LEA & PERRINS WORCESTERSHIRE SAUCE, first imported into the U. S. in 1849, is one of the most prevalent identifiable food related bottles in the Leadville area from the 1800's.

Either the product was well liked or it was used to cover the taste of whatever else was being eaten.

The example on the right is 5ozs. They came in all sizes at least up to 32ozs. One plus about flavor for the canned food industry of the time is that no **LEA & PERRINS** bottles were found with the cans.

This bottle on the right has an embossed glass stopper wrapped in cork.

The other choice, besides cans, to pack preserved food was in glass containers. Below are a few samples of the thousands of varieties of food bottles used in the 1800's. They were sealed either with a glass stopper or a cork.

The embossed one is **MELLIN'S FOOD** of **BOSTON, U. S. A.** This is the large size of the baby food product. They registered their label on Dec. 20, 1881.

The second bottle from the left contained pickles from the **H. J. HEINZ CO.**

The deep blue bottle on the left had been discarded, like many others, in one of the hundreds of privies that lined the alleys before indoor plumbing.

Thousands of **BROMO-SELTZER** bottles were thrown away over the years and fragments of blue are still seen wherever old glass was discarded. Now and again some perfect examples are still found.

The pestle on the right was found laying on the ground during telephone cable burying operations in 1965 at Buena Vista, Colorado. Seven years later I noticed the mortar on a shelf at a gas station in Eagle, Colorado. I was told it was dug up at the old Leadville dump. We decided my half was probably the rarer of the two, and I had some bottles the owner was interested in, so we traded. Glass made before World War I, that contained the chemical Manganese Dioxide, turns purple when exposed to sunlight.

The pestle and mortar were valued at $200 by the appraisers at The Antiques Roadshow.

There was no shortage of medicines to cure just about everything. The green bottle contained **LACTOPEPTINE FOR ALL DIGESTIVE AILMENTS.**

The amber bottle was **Garfield Digestive Tablets.** These seemed fitting additions for the trial and error methods of early food preserving. These are the earliest screw top bottles, and are called ground top bottles.

The clear bottle contained **DR. PIERCES ANURIC TABLETS FOR KIDNEY'S AND BACKACHE.** It was sealed with a cork. All were dug from our backyard. The thin dime shows size.

Because most outbuildings have been torn down or burned over the years it's difficult to know their original purpose. The barn still standing in the backyard of the home we owned for sixteen years was multi-purposed. It was used for animals, including chickens. It had a laundry room with a wood stove. It was used for coal and wood storage. It also contained two indoor outhouses, one of which was finished with wainscoting.

The middle and far right (**PATENTED APRIL '3D', 1900),** whiskey bottles, along with more than 30 others, were found under a loose board on the barn floor in the hallway leading to one of the indoor outhouses.

The smaller whiskey, one quarter pint, was purchased for its color and spider web design. It says in part: '**ANTIQUE** Brand, Spring of 1914, the Frankfort Distillery, Kentucky. For medicinal purposes only.' They called it 'a 100 proof alcoholic stimulant.'

The first two whiskey bottles on the right were among the 30 other bottles found under the barn floor. I don't know how unusual they all are, but when you find 30 together they appear quite common.

The **QUAKER MAID WHISKEY** is quite fancy.

The **1886 DUFFY MALT WHISKEY of ROCHESTER, N. Y.** can be found in many shops. They are an attractive bottle.

The **RED TOP** bottle is collectable because of the embossed **TOP**.

An observation made in regards to one habit that most of the drinkers of that time period had was that they invariably put the cork or stopper back on the bottle before throwing it away. Most medicine bottles had their corks in place also. Whatever their reason, it kept the inside of the bottle relatively clean.

The miniature below, **'Compliments of M. MAL-LETTE, MILACA,—MINN.'** in perfect condition, is an example of an extremely collectable item. This rare size, with a value of about $125, was discovered in 2004 in a thrift store for 99 cents. These were made in the 1890's and given out as samples by merchants for early advertising.

Bargains like this are still found on rare occasions by diligent searchers of antiques. It's usually a case of being in the right place at the right time. The thrill of the hunt spurs collectors on.

The miniature in comparison to the one gallon whiskey jugs.

On the right are three examples of the highly collectable cobalt stamped whiskey jugs from Leadville. They were sold as a throw away item in the latter 1800's and early 1900's. Today they sell for hundreds of dollars depending on rarity, size and condition. The **SCHLOSS BROS** was found under a house. There were more than fifteen establishments in Leadville that had their names stamped on various sizes and shapes of whiskey jugs.

Collecting things from the past makes history come alive. The 'pot lid' below was found in an antique store in Lynden, Washington. Later, we were viewing the Titanic exhibit in Seattle. Among the relics retrieved from the ocean floor was a 'pot lid' like this one that we had already found. A few special items had been reproduced for sale as souvenirs in their gift shop, one of which was a container with the same pot-lid as the one shown here. The originals are transfer ware on ironstone.

The part that makes it exciting for us as collectors is to find that something we had already chosen to have, among our own collectibles, is also historically significant.

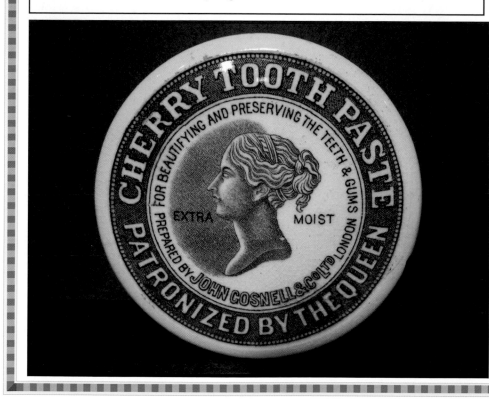

The 'pot lid' above was the first one we found that introduced us to the variety of detail on 'pot lids.' Like so many of the discarded collectables featured in this book, this also was at the bottom of an outhouse. This one made it all the way from Paris.

Before indoor plumbing, chamber pots were in most homes to eliminate a night-time run to the cold outdoors. This is an example of early red transfer ware. No matter how lowly the purpose of a vessel was, people wanted beauty.

This was found at a depth of six feet while digging up an early outhouse. The base was found first, afterwards the lid was located a few inches lower. It was probably discarded because of the broken handle, which wasn't found.

The chamber pot is stamped with a trademark from England. The trademark has a **CROWN** and the names **J. H. DAVIS**, and **CHATSWORTH.**

The other discarded things found at this depth were the two embossed Budweiser bottles, the deep blue bottle, medicine bottles, a pair of china doll arms and the brass bell. It is usual when digging these old outhouses to find very little in the first four or five feet.

The brass bell was just an inch above the chamber pot, which should have broken the pot when dropped in.

TWO COMMON HOUSEHOLD ITEMS

Quite a number of individuals dig the old outhouses as a hobby, others dig them for their own collections and still others in the hopes of finding something valuable to sell. I don't know if many do it for historical reasons, other than for determining value.

Only after starting to research the history of the labels did I realize how much other history we had accumulated. The pitcher on the left was dug out of our backyard in pieces during foundation work. It became evident, because of the soft ground, that where I was trying to place a foundation there was an old outhouse. Therefore I needed to dig down until I hit solid ground. That was six feet later. A number of bottles and lots of pieces of white china were found in that six feet of dirt. The last piece found was the large piece with part of the rim. It was then that I decided to try to put it back together. I had found all but two small pieces out of thirty.

It is **ROYAL IRONSTONE CHINA** by **ALFRED MEAKIN. LONDON.** It makes a good conversation piece.

Old irons are uncovered regularly in many places.

The unusual **sleeve iron** below was found while digging on another foundation job.

The train on the two and a quarter inch watch case on the right is very similar to the seven inch cast iron toy below. The toy train was dug up while digging a hole for a fence post in 1966. They are a reminder of the mode of transportation that enabled the canned foods to arrive in Leadville.

The four inch long toy roofers hatchet was under the edge of another home in the dirt. The smaller one was for advertising. Engraved on the handle is **FLORENCE'S HATCHET.** One half inch of its handle was sticking out of the ground at the old Leadville dump.

These three cast iron toys were found under houses. The horse and race car had been dropped under a stairway and then they slid down until they wedged against a brick chimney. They were recovered from the dry area at the base of the chimney when it was removed.

The trolley car was laying in the dirt under another house.

Walking in any area where people lived and worked over a period of years yields small traces of their lives. One arm, leg or a small head may be all that remains of a doll that was enjoyed by some long forgotten child of years gone by.

When you find remnants of discarded dolls it makes you wonder at what point in the dolls wear and tear it was decided to throw it away, and who made that decision?

You can find examples of many of these dolls at antique stores and shows, but it's not quite the same as finding scattered remnants and contemplating about the long ago lives of the original owner. The 1892 dime was in the dirt under our home, and makes a good gauge for the size of other objects.

All of these doll parts were found by just walking along various locations. Usually only one tiny piece is seen, and the rest must be carefully uncovered so as to not damage it any further. You get the feeling of discovery that must be the experience of an archeologist.

One characteristic that stands out is that the lips, cheeks, eyes, shoes, and hair have retained their color after being in the ground, in most cases for over 100 years.

Some of the various shapes and sizes of doll pieces.

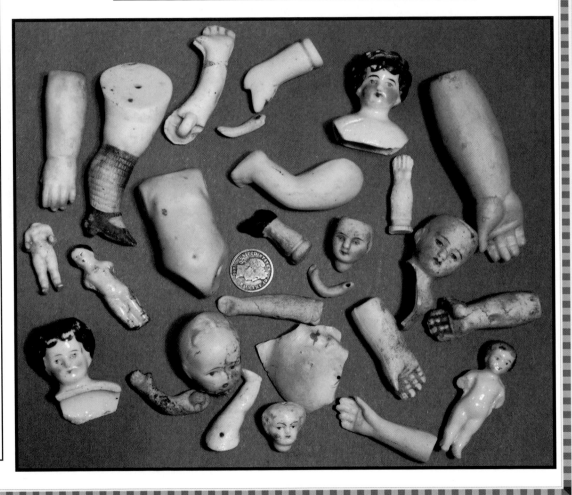

All of these China Doll heads from Germany were found buried in the ground, in various locations.

Their age can be known by the shape of the face. They were hand painted, so all are different.

Finding items used by children reminds us that families quickly followed the miners into the camps and civilized them. The miners and the camps.

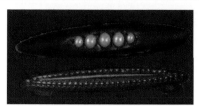

These one inch long bar pins had been lost or discarded. It seems the smaller that something is, the more exciting it can be when you find it.

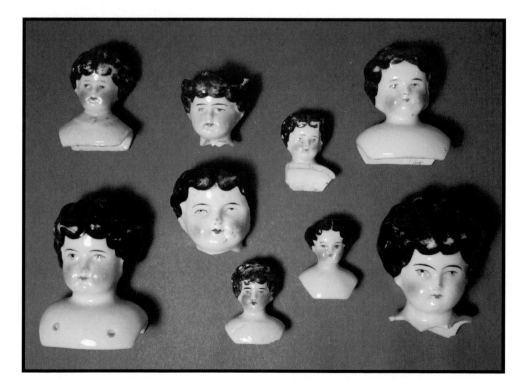

Shoes are one of the most common items discarded under homes. The vast majority don't get much attention, but on occasion one is interesting enough to haul home. This button top baby shoe is an example. The durability of leather is quite remarkable.

Earlier in the book it was mentioned that a local resident was picking up bottles that were being uncovered as we were burying a telephone cable, and her husband was sifting an older part of the dump. Later we became good friends for many years with Horace and Jean Curnutt. These discarded souvenirs of past events were among the many things he found while sifting.

Three were from the **CRYSTAL CARNIVAL** of **1895 & 1896.** On the middle right two smelter workers and a stack of silver bars are shown on the one side.

The one on the bottom left is the **FOURTH** of **JULY CARNIVAL of 1900,** and the one on the bottom right is the **PARIS EXPOSITION** of **1889.** The Eiffel tower can be seen on its lower right.

The advertising token above was sifted from the old dump. It was for **HIGH GRADE BUGGIES** From the **PARRY MFG. CO. INDIANAPOLIS**

The identification tag on the right came from the same source. I was told by a serious collector of this type of memorabilia that the T. & W. stood for Tabor and Waddell. Tabor was Silver King Horace A. W. Tabor. Waddell was William B. Waddell, of Russell, Majors & Waddell, the organizers of the Pony Express. This endeavor would have had to be before Tabor came to Leadville in 1877, because Waddell died in 1872. It's possible to have been from the 1860's, or early 1870's.

Only three of these tags are known to exist.

This early child's cup was found with the 1890's cans. The illustration must depict some nursery rhyme or other story from the past, but none I have found fits the entire illustration. The girls expression looks like **Mistress Mary Quite Contrary**, but the scene is a seashore instead of a garden.

What makes this more interesting is that the one old cup I found in the highest incorporated town in the U. S. is a scene from the seashore.

These souvenirs from 1895-96, show the largest **ICE PALACE** ever built. It was constructed in a little over a month by about 300 laborers and craftsmen.

After the **ICE PALACE** melted in 1896, the lumber that had been used for the roof, window frames, and outbuildings was now used to construct barracks to house troops brought in to quell a strike.

After they left, the barracks were dismantled and the lumber was used again in the construction of several houses. One of these is now **THE ICE PALACE INN, Bed & Breakfast.**

During renovations at the **THE ICE PALACE INN** in 2004, the sign above was found pasted on an exterior board under the original siding. Whether it was giving directions at the original Ice Palace or at the later barracks can't be ascertained, but it did prove that in the latter 1890's lumber was being recycled.

The one inch tall pewter child's teapot, also seen on the cover, was found with the aid of my six year old grandson, McKaulay. The very top of the handle was seen sticking out of the ground, and McKaulay carefully pulled it out. It reminded us of the teapot from 'Beauty and the Beast.' Finding items from the past, that we are able to relate to, makes history live, no matter whether we are young or old.

Photos this page - Kami Kolakowski

Two rare etched souvenir teaspoons from the
1896 LEADVILLE ICE PALACE.

From what I have heard this was a road sign placed along the pony express route in the 1940's. They were stolen about as fast as they were put up. This one remained long enough to get shot three times. It was retrieved from the trash of the highway department in the 1940's.

As shown on the sign the Pony Express operated for two years. It was from April 1860 to November 1861. They began carrying 20 pounds of mail at $5.00 per 1/2 oz., and ended carrying it for $1.00 per 1/2 oz.

The route was between St. Joseph, Missouri, and Sacramento, California. They followed the same route taken in 1846 by the ill-fated Donner party.

The Donner party spent six months on the trail and five months snowed in before the last survivor was brought to Sutters Fort, California. The Pony Express made it in ten days. As soon as the telegraph was completed to California on October 24, 1861, the Pony Express, which never made a profit, stopped operations.

The route taken by the Donner party and the Pony Express was not the same route as the California Trail. The route they took left the California Trail and turned southward at Fort Bridger, Wyoming, passing south of the Great Salt Lake, and joined the California Trail near Wells, Nevada. My great, great grandfather Thomas Rhoades, with his wife Elizabeth and fourteen children, was with the Donner group until they reached Fort Bridger, where an argument ensued over which route should be taken. This resulted in the Rhoades party staying on the longer route through Fort Hall, Idaho.

They arrived at Sutters Fort, California in September without incident, expecting the Donner group to already be there. Not until February 1847, did word get through about the ongoing tragedy. The first rescue party of seven men included the two oldest Rhoades boys, John and Daniel.

The route known as the Hastings cutoff, a shortcut for a man on a horse, and later used by the Pony Express, proved very costly for families, teams and wagons.

Invariably, whenever I would tell about things or show individuals treasures I had found during remodeling, the question asked would be: "But did you find any money?" Finally after 1985, I was able to answer "Yes!" During the renovations of one room that would become our new kitchen we were removing the old linoleum. Under the third and final layer in one corner was this folded envelope. Inside the envelope, with the date July 16, 1927, was this **TEN DOLLAR** bill. It was hidden there after 1927 and before the new owners bought the house in 1931. Likely the hiding of the ten dollars was tied into the stock market crash of 1929. The year 1929 was also the year the size of currency was reduced to the familiar size we use today.

This ten dollar bill was well circulated by the time it was hidden, but it did last longer than the average life span for paper money, which today is eighteen months for a ten dollar bill. It has twelve tack holes in it from installation of the three layers of linoleum. It is the series of 1914, and says it is redeemable in gold. In uncirculated condition it would be worth about $35. As is, it is worth $10.

They could have hidden a ten dollar gold piece instead. It wouldn't have been any more at the time, but would be worth over $300 today.

Money is quite often found during the restoration of old homes, but not usually the ones I worked on.

A partial display of the older labeled cans and drugstore related items.

In the few years since the discovery of these old labels, one thing stood out. The more I looked for information about them, the less I found had ever been written about the early food labels. By the time some of the major food processing corporations began to save and display their procession of labels, the earlier ones were gone. The best display that I found on a website is of the Del-Monte Brand. The first label displayed is from 1909. Some older black and white images of labels are seen, one from 1886, but it's not known whether these exist as actual labels. Most of the California and Utah labels in this book became a part of the Del-Monte Company.

My initial reason to research the labels was motivated by a desire to know if they were worth anything. After a short time it was evident they are very rare, but their history and beauty have proven to be far more important than their monetary value.

At the Antiques Roadshow the value for the collection shown on page V was placed, at the time, between $10,000 and $14,000.

I expected more labeled cans to show up after the cans were shown on P.B.S., but they haven't.

What the final value will prove to be only time will tell. For now, at least, the labels and their history have been recorded and preserved in this book.

****

As reported in 'Antique Weekly,' a beer can found in the rafters of a building, for CLIPPER PALE BEER, having a picture of Boeings trans-oceanic 'flying boat' Yankee Clipper, sold on eBay on December 2, 2002, for $19,300.

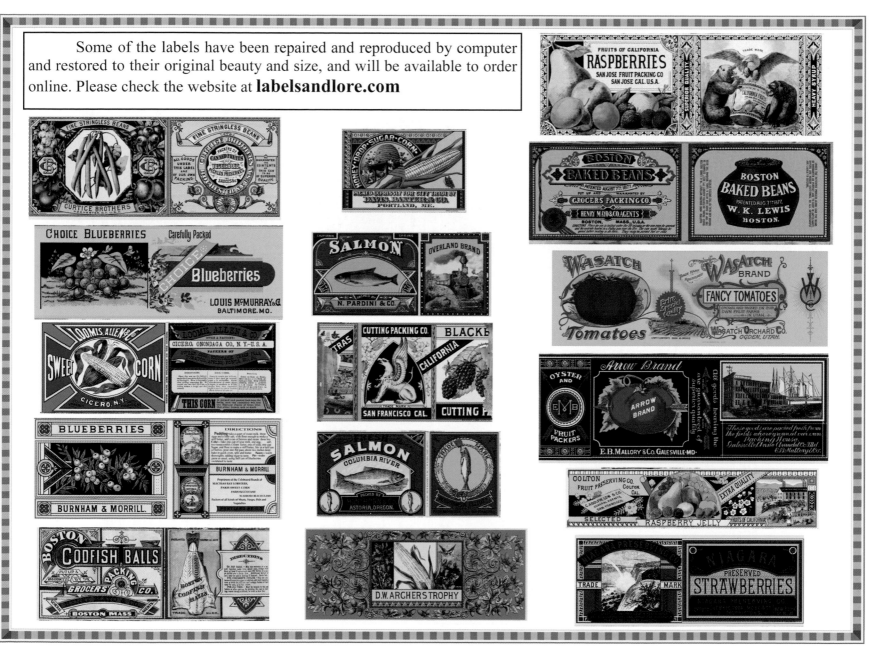

Two examples of the restored labels (shown smaller than the actual size)

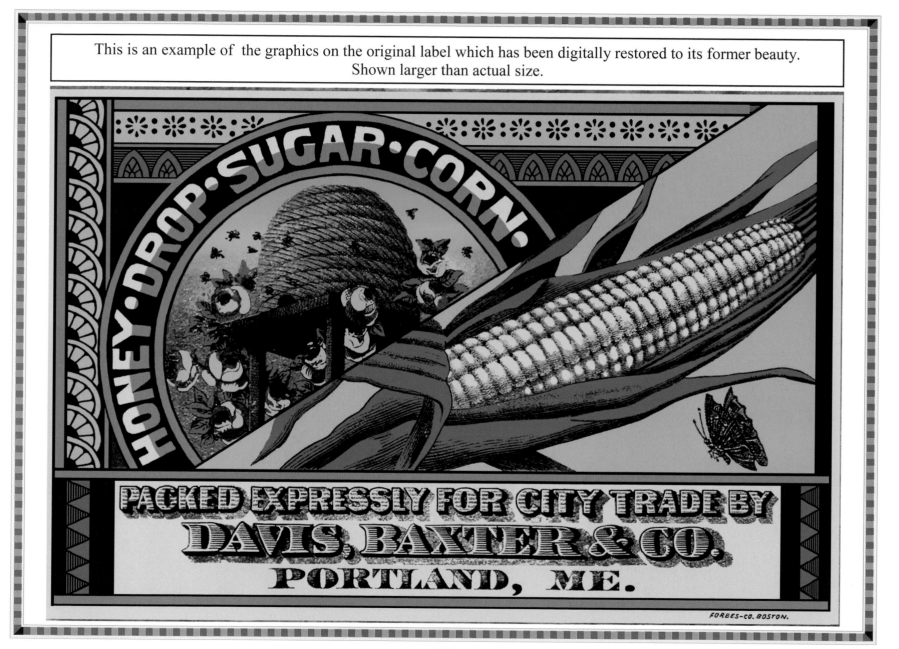

183

AUTHOR'S EARLY TRAVELS

1. Acapulco, Mexico   -   1946
2. Galveston, Texas   -   1947
3. Olympic National Park, WA   -   1949
4. Tucson, Arizona   -   1948
5. Yosemite, California -   1949
6. Vanderhoof, British Columbia   -   1952
7. Niagara Falls, New York   -   1953
8. Mammoth Cave, Kentucky   -   1953